THE NEW SHAME
OF THE CITIES

BY JOHN PERAZZO

Introduction

American politics is dominated by an enduring myth—that Democrats are the party of the common man; the voiceless, the powerless, the poor. That if you care about what happens to the least among us, you will cast your vote in the Democratic column.

But the reality is this: the vast majority of voiceless, powerless and poor people are concentrated in Detroit, Philadelphia, St. Louis, Chicago, Atlanta, and America's other large urban centers. All of them are run by Democrats and have been for 50 to 100 years. On the Democrats' watch, these cities have become the equivalent of holding cells for the poor and minorities. Everything that's wrong with America's cities that can be affected by policy, Democrats are responsible for. There are poor to be helped, but Democrats have buried them deeper in poverty and powerlessness. There are minorities who seek opportunities, but Democrats have kept them second class citizens. Democrats have been the problem rather than the solution.

In 1904, Lincoln Steffens, a major figure in the group of journalists Teddy Roosevelt called "muckrakers," published a groundbreaking book called *Shame of the Cities*. In it he examined the inner workings of America's great urban centers and found them swarming with graft and corruption. In his searing portraits of these cities, Steffens documented the inner workings of political machines across the country which were then imitating the apparatus built a few decades earlier by Tammany Hall's notorious Boss Tweed, first of this new breed of crooked backroom Democratic princes of the city. Steffens showed how these machines ran over and flattened the lives of ordinary working people. But even more than corruption itself, Steffens was incensed by the complicity of intellectuals and opinion makers—people who knew that the political machines mangled democracy but had nonetheless allowed them to make America's cities cesspools of poverty and despair.

If Lincoln Steffens was alive today, he would feel even greater outrage at the current disastrous state of America's cities, as documented by John Perrazo in *The New Shame of the Cities*. Steffens would see in Perrazo's portraits of the present-day machines of the Democrat Party, which have ruled America's cities for a generation, today's equivalent of Tammany Hall. He would see their governance not simply as an expression of failed policies, but as a massive human rights violation that has delivered the poor and minorities into a state of hopelessness and made them a permanent underclass. And, as he did in his own time, Steffens would feel contempt for today's political class that has stood by and watched this urban tragedy unfold and bought into the Democrats' myth that they are actually protectors of the poor.

It didn't have to turn out this way. In part because of the issues Steffens himself raised at the turn of the twentieth century, good government movements took hold with the goal of making municipal government responsible and efficient and the cities themselves livable. By the 1930s, the metropolises of the United States had become centers of enterprise, commerce, and culture—"big shouldered," in the phrase Carl Sandburg used to describe bustling Chicago, one of the most industrious—as they integrated a generation of new immigrants into the national fabric and welcomed the businesses and corporations that provided paychecks for workers and prosperity for the nation.

To be sure, the great American cities of the early 20th century were run for the most part by politicians whose allegiance was to the New Deal, many of them autocrats who held office for decades. But these politicians were judged on how well their policies produced real-life solutions for the poor and how well they advanced the poor into the middle class. Voters and residents were interested only in one thing: whether or not the cities these politicians managed "worked."

That was then and this is now. As John Perazzo shows in *The New Shame of the Cities*, over the last fifty years America's urban centers have slid into a violence, corruption and savage dysfunction that make the snapshots of despair Lincoln Steffens produced at the beginning of the 20th century seem mild by comparison. The cities that were once the engines powering the American Century have stopped functioning. Going back to the future, they are once again America's shame.

From Atlanta to Newark and Washington D.C. to St. Louis, Perazzo shows how contemporary urban life has become stuck in reverse, bankrupt in finance and in spirit.

"Detroit, ruled by Democrats for nearly a half century, has hemorrhaged population, becoming a ghost town," he writes, "as it has gone from being the automotive capital of America, producer of its dream machines, to the murder capital—according to *Forbes* magazine, the most dangerous city in the country." About Baltimore, also governed by the Democratic Party for more than 50 years, the verdict is equally grim: "As a result of widespread political corruption, a damaged economy, astronomically high taxes, and escalating crime rates, population fell by 120,000 just in the 1990s, making the city blacker and poorer. Tens of thousands of homes were simply abandoned by residents desperate to escape." The verdict on Chicago is rendered by its new street nickname "Chiraq," a reference to the killings that have become commonplace and know no holiday truce: there were 45 shootings in the city on Easter weekend 2014 alone, six of the victims children.

Perrazo's portraits of these once great American metropolises show how Democratic Party policies have made them into little more than holding cells for blacks and Hispanics and other minorities immiserated by the policies of their Democratic Party rulers. This urban tragedy isn't the result of some impersonal historical process; nor is it, as the Democrats who have presided over the catastrophe like to claim, caused by racism or neglect by the federal government. The reasons for the decline of America's cities are indeed complicated, but there should be no argument that it has occurred as a result of policies designed and implemented by the Democrats, or that this decline began in the 1960s, when the pragmatic centrists who had defined the Democratic Party for a generation and had built livable cities were defeated by "new politics" liberals, soon to label themselves "progressives," who proceeded to make these cities into mad laboratories for their leftist ideological experiments.

Today's Democrat power brokers have monopolized power even more ruthlessly than the bosses Lincoln Steffens targeted in his exposé over a hundred years ago (while piously claiming that they do so for "the people" in a way that even those otherwise shameless politicians would have considered hypocritical). They believe that the measure of a city's administration is no longer whether it creates solutions that "work" or whether most of its residents' lives are improving most of the time. Instead, success is now determined by the size of the municipal bureaucracy and the power it has over every aspect of individual lives; by scapegoating and stigmatization of the "greedy" businesses that had traditionally created the jobs providing each new American generation with greater social and financial opportunities than the previous one had enjoyed; by mortgaging the educational system, which once offered poor people their best opportunity to step out of caste, to the teachers' unions which in return keep the political status quo in place with their money and votes.

The fiscal irresponsibility that has driven our cities to bankruptcy has daily, real-life, real-time consequences for citizens as budgets are slashed and first responders are cut back. "When Detroit residents place a call seeking help from the city's understaffed police department," Perazzo writes, "they must wait an average of 58 minutes for an officer to arrive at the scene."

Today's big-city Democrats, while utter failures at bettering the lives of their constituents, are very good at the class warfare rhetoric and conspiracy theories that make these constituents feel that the Party that has beaten them down is actually their last best hope. This is why Democrats routinely receive over 90% of the votes in elections whose nearly unanimous results call to mind those that once took place in the Soviet bloc.

In the background of Perazzo's profiles of corruption and malfeasance that is literally criminal—America's big-city mayors and administrators over the last several decades have gone to jail in astounding numbers—are national policies that have trickled down despair to the cities and to the African American and Hispanic poor, whom Democrats still cynically claim to protect. Welfare programs promoted since the 1960s by successive Democrat administrations in our urban centers have created the perverse incentives that lead to three quarters of black children being born out of wedlock and growing up in families without fathers; an outcome that haunts the community later on, since fatherless young black males commit crimes, most of them against other blacks, at astronomic rates. Access to subprime housing loans and lax lending standards promoted in the name of "social justice" during the 1990s by Democrat city and federal governments and by radical allies such as ACORN, caused the collapse of the national housing market that hit these minorities twice as hard as it hit whites and led to a huge reduction in family wealth among blacks and Hispanics.

The New Shame of the Cities shows the same grim

picture in city after city, where the poor have gotten poorer and the whites have moved away over the last generation, creating ghost neighborhoods where abandoned homes stand like pulled teeth. But what has been a catastrophe for the people unfortunate enough to still have to live in such places (a recent poll by the *Detroit Free Press* found that 40% of the city's population, drastically reduced over the last 50 years, planned to move as soon as possible) has been a godsend for the Democrats in charge. *Forbes* magazine summarizes the moral of the story: "A politician or a political party can achieve long-term dominance by tipping the balance of votes in their direction through the implementation of policies that strangle and stifle economic growth. Counterintuitively, making a city poorer leads to political success for the engineers of that impoverishment."[1] It is also a story with a cynical twist: most of these failing cities are now administered by black Democrats, which means that anyone criticizing their failed policies can be attacked as "racist." Incompetent at everything else, these politicians have become adept at projecting blame onto the abstract other—Washington, exploitive businesses and businessmen, "white flight," racism.

The statistics that Perrazo has assembled in this work, drearily similar in city after city, have the cumulative power of a punch in the face: Black unemployment at 16.3 percent (19.1 percent for young black males). Poverty rates of 37.5 percent and 35.5 percent, respectively, for Hispanic and black single parents. Sixty percent of rapists, 72 percent of adolescent murderers, and 70 percent of long-

---

[1] http://www.forbes.com/sites/markhendrickson/2012/05/31/president-obamas-wealth-destroying-goal-taking-the-curley-effect-nationwide/

term prisoners, are men who grew up in fatherless families encouraged by Democratic welfare programs. And public school, once the way out, now a dead end with 45 percent and 43 percent of black and Hispanic students dropping out at a time when those who fail to graduate from high school in America earn only about half as much as those who do.

This urban chamber of horrors has been built on the watch of Democratic Party city governments, often with black mayors, who have helped turn our once-proud big cities into the equivalent of black reservations. African American sociologist Walter E. Williams had it exactly right when he once surveyed this urban wreckage and said, "The welfare state has done to black Americans what slavery couldn't do, what Jim Crow couldn't do, what the harshest racism couldn't do. And that is to destroy the black family."[2]

The New Shame of the Cities gives the lie to the liberal idea—never anything more than a power grab disguised as compassion—that it takes a government to elevate an individual. By documenting the ruinous state of our once great cities, this work illumines a darker truth: that it takes a government to destroy the communities that give individual life dignity and purpose.

--Peter Collier

---

[2] http://online.wsj.com/news/articles/SB10001424052748704881304576094221050061598

Detroit

Hard as it is to believe today—when Detroit has the desolate, bombed-out look of a conquered nation—fifty years ago there were few more exciting and attractive places for Americans, black and white, to live. As the social critic Matthew Josephson observed in the 1920s, when the city was on the move: "Nowhere in the world may the trend of the new industrial cycle be perceived more clearly than in Detroit. In this sense, it is the most modern city in the world, the city of tomorrow."[3] University of Michigan historian Jeffrey Mirel puts it this way: "Throughout the 1920s, Detroit was the shining star of the new era, the very center of the American economic universe, where capitalism and technology combined to produce the greatest goods for the greatest numbers."[4]

Detroit is best known as the home of the "Big Three" auto makers—General Motors, Ford, and Chrysler—who made the U.S. and the rest of the world mobile and powered what at the time seemed an urban research-and-demonstration project. During the decades of the early to mid twentieth century, the auto industry's need for massive quantities of steel, glass, copper, and (later) plastic gave rise to numerous enterprises related to car manufacture that employed hundreds of thousands of additional blue-collar

---

[3] http://books.google.com/books?id=5ceGeWusD7gC&pg=PA217&source=gbs_toc_r&cad=3#v=onepage&q&f=false

[4] http://books.google.com/books?id=5ceGeWusD7gC&pg=PA217&source=gbs_toc_r&cad=3#v=onepage&q&f=false

workers in and around the city.⁵ The assembly line was perfected here, and brought with it the idea that industrial workers could expect to enjoy a middle-class lifestyle.

During World War II, Detroit was a key part of the arsenal of democracy, producing tanks, jeeps and a host of other weapons that helped win the war. In the postwar years the city boomed, building the tail-finned, futuristic cars that in turn symbolized the American Dream—of mobility, financial stability, and success. By the 1950s, Detroit had become the fifth largest city in the United States, home to nearly two million residents.⁶ By 1960, it had the highest per capita income of any city in the country.⁷

As the Sixties progressed, Motown Records—founded in Detroit by one of its native sons, Berry Gordy Jr.—produced such megastars as Diana Ross and the Supremes, Marvin Gaye, the Jackson Five, the Temptations, the Four Tops, the Commodores, and Gladys Knight & the Pips, who made the music America hummed. The city school system, meanwhile, turned out capable graduates.

The Sixties was also the moment when Detroit began to experience its reversal of fortune. The city was hit particularly hard by the social turbulence of this revolutionary era, most notably a rising militancy among local community

---

⁵ http://www.gilderlehrman.org/history-by-era/politics-reform/essays/motor-city-story-detroit

⁶ http://www.gilderlehrman.org/history-by-era/politics-reform/essays/motor-city-story-detroit

⁷ http://www.nationalreview.com/article/353862/detroit-goes-down-kevin-d-williamson

organizers angered by what they perceived to be the slow pace of civil-rights reforms[8]—although Detroit had a large and prosperous black middle class, higher-than-normal wages for unskilled black workers because of the auto industry, and two black U.S. congressmen. Moreover, Detroit had acquired millions in federal funds through President Lyndon Johnson's Great Society programs and invested them almost exclusively in the inner city, where poverty and social problems were concentrated. The *Washington Post* claimed that Detroit's inner-city schools were undergoing "the country's leading and most forceful reforms in education."[9] Housing conditions were not viewed as worse than those of other Northern cities. In 1965, the American Institute of Architects gave Detroit an award for urban redevelopment.[10]

Nonetheless, Rev. Albert Cleague and other Detroit-area activists openly called for black separatism and self-determination on the premise that whites would never voluntarily choose to share political power with blacks.[11] At a July 1967 Black Power rally in Detroit, the radical H. Rap Brown gave voice to the city's growing unrest when he warned "Motown" that if it did not make sufficient reforms, "we are going to burn you down."[12]

---

[8] http://tinyurl.com/ktf3564

[9] http://www.dailykos.com/story/2013/07/27/1227025/-Detroit-s-Long-Road-to-Bankruptcy-Began-Because-of-Resentment-Towards-it-s-First-Black-Mayor#

[10] http://tinyurl.com/mxguzry

[11] http://tinyurl.com/ktf3564

[12] http://tinyurl.com/km2993h

This inflammatory racial discontent grew at a time when the Democratic Party, claiming to be sensitive to the problems of minorities, was completing a takeover of city government. In 1961, the reins of political power in the city fell permanently into Democrats' hands. In the 53 years that have passed since then, Detroit has not had a single Republican mayor. Indeed, it has elected only one Republican to its City Council since 1970.[13] As it was becoming a failed city, it was also becoming a political monoculture.

The first mayor of Detroit's Democratic Party era, Jerome Cavanagh (1962-70), was a white liberal who greatly expanded the role of government in the city and took pains to appoint blacks to prominent positions in his administration.[14]

Cavanagh also served on the "Model Cities" task force that President Johnson launched in 1966 as part of his Great Society and War on Poverty programs. Although it distantly echoed Soviet efforts to rebuild urban areas in Eastern Europe, this centralized approach to urban development was seen in the '60s as the hallmark of a new era. Along with United Auto Workers president Walter Reuther, Cavanagh persuaded President Johnson to designate a nine-square-mile section of Detroit—an area where 134,000 people (one-ninth of the city's population) resided—as a pilot

---

[13] http://nation.foxnews.com/2013/07/22/how-democrats-and-unions-destroyed-detroit

[14] http://dailyreckoning.com/detroits-socialist-nightmare-is-americas-future/

location for the Model Cities initiative.[15] The overriding objective of Model Cities was to demonstrate the amazing ability of federal grants to rehabilitate slums and replace them with publicly financed "affordable housing"; alleviate poverty by injecting rivers of taxpayer money into social programs; provide ghetto dwellers with federally funded jobs at municipal and nonprofit agencies; and create a host of job-training, healthcare, educational, and recreational facilities for the poor.[16] In just a few short years, $490 million in federal funds were poured into Detroit to bankroll these programs.[17] On top of this, Cavanaugh was able to get Michigan's state legislature to pass new taxes that would help pay for the Model Cities program and would be borne entirely by "the rich."[18]

The government giveaways not only failed in their immediate goals of creating changes that would lead to upward social mobility, but actually fostered resentment at the paternalism at the heart of the Model Cities program— the idea that "disadvantaged" people's decisions about where they could live, where they could build businesses, and how they should run those enterprises should be

---

[15] http://www.detroits-great-rebellion.com/Miriani-Crackdown.html; http://books.google.com/books?id=c_LpEOQMEq4C&pg=PA111&lpg=PA111&dq=#v=onepage&q&f=false

[16] http://www.detroits-great-rebellion.com/Miriani-Crackdown.html; http://www.frontpagemag.com/2013/arnold-ahlert/toxic-government-by-democrats-detroit-2/; http://www.detroityes.com/mb/showthread.php?12355-This-week-in-Detroit-City-History-1968-Federal-quot-Model-Cities-quot-program

[17] http://detroitplanninghistory.weebly.com/jerome-cavanagh-elected-mayor.html

[18] http://www.frontpagemag.com/2013/arnold-ahlert/how-the-democrats-destroyed-detroit/

micromanaged by a bureaucratic elite.[19]

In the final analysis, for all the hugger mugger at its launching, Detroit's Model City program and the half-a-billion taxpayer dollars that funded it purchased very little in terms of urban regeneration. Some contend that the program "worked," in the sense that it temporarily—albeit at an unsustainable cost—decreased poverty and unemployment slightly in the targeted communities. But instead of encouraging entrepreneurship and self-reliance, it mainly promoted dependence on government and thus led to no lasting gains for its "beneficiaries." By 1990, Detroit's Model City area had lost 63% of its population and 45% of its housing units, statistics that rendered a sobering verdict on the program.[20]

Mayor Cavanaugh's political and economic policies not only failed to resuscitate Detroit's blighted neighborhoods, but also intensified the percolating rage of local black militants. Every guilty gesture of appeasement and recompense made by the Democratic city administration only increased radicals' indignation about the condescending inadequacy of those gestures and stoked the fires of a "revolution of rising expectations." And then, in July 1967, H. Rap Brown's threat became a reality as Detroit was set on fire by radicals, becoming the scene of the decade's most horrific urban race riot—43 deaths, 1,200 injuries, over 7,200 arrests, and more than

---

[19] http://dailyreckoning.com/detroits-socialist-nightmare-is-americas-future/

[20] http://books.google.com/books?id=c_LpEOQMEq4C&pg=PA111&lpg=PA111&dq=#v=onepage&q&f=false

2,000 buildings destroyed.[21] This calamity would continue to resonate in the years to come as a massive "white flight" that led some 140,000 people to evacuate the central city within a mere 18 months. Detroit would never be the same again.[22]

By now the Democratic Party—increasingly radicalized by the growing influence of the New Left—was making the city into a laboratory experiment for destructive urban policies. In 1974, Democrat Coleman Young, a secret member of the Communist Party, began a 20-year stint as Detroit's first black mayor. Scholar Steven Malanga writes that Young, from an economic standpoint, "lacked a plan except to go to war with the city's major institutions and demand that the federal government save it with subsidies"—a strategy that critics referred to as "tin-cup urbanism."[23] Under Young's disastrous stewardship, Detroit's debt rating reached junk status.[24] By 1987, 34% of Detroit residents were on welfare rolls—more than 4 times as many as in 1967.[25] During that same two-decade period, nearly 200,000 jobs were lost in the city.[26] The late political scientist James Q. Wilson wrote that by the

---

[21] http://www.frontpagemag.com/2013/arnold-ahlert/how-the-democrats-destroyed-detroit/

[22] http://www.frontpagemag.com/2013/arnold-ahlert/toxic-government-by-democrats-detroit-2/

[23] http://online.wsj.com/news/articles/SB10001424127887324110404578625581152645480

[24] http://www.washingtonpost.com/blogs/on-leadership/wp/2013/07/19/what-killed-detroit-lets-not-forget-the-who/;

[25] http://tinyurl.com/k8e8vfz

[26] http://tinyurl.com/k8e8vfz

end of Young's mayoralty, Detroit was "a fiscal and social wreck."[27]

Young also further poisoned the waters of black-white relations in Detroit, routinely playing the race card to maintain his hold on city hall by engaging in an "us-against-them" style of politics that essentially branded anyone who opposed him as a "racist."[28] This tactic increased racial polarization, drove multitudes of whites out of the city, and helped plunge Detroit ever deeper into social and economic chaos.[29] *TIME* editor Daniel Okrent has portrayed Young's mayoralty as the "corrosive two-decade rule of a black politician who cared more about retribution than about resurrection."[30] The *Washington Post*, similarly, describes Young as someone who promoted "racial divisiveness" and "did little to try and mend fences broken down along racial lines."[31]

Nowhere was this more apparent than in Young's policies vis à vis law-enforcement. Dividing his city's police department along racial lines, the mayor created separate layoff lists for white and black officers. Young made it clear, moreover, that policing practices which resulted in

---

[27] http://online.wsj.com/news/articles/SB10001424127887324110404578625581152645480

[28] http://news.google.com/newspapers?nid=1350&dat=19930626&id=lVdPAAAAIBAJ&sjid=VAMEAAAAIBAJ&pg=6310,6814490

[29] http://www.examiner.com/article/detroit-s-collapse-the-young-years

[30] http://www.washingtonpost.com/blogs/on-leadership/wp/2013/07/19/what-killed-detroit-lets-not-forget-the-who/

[31] http://www.washingtonpost.com/blogs/on-leadership/wp/2013/07/19/what-killed-detroit-lets-not-forget-the-who/

disproportionately high numbers of arrests or citations of African Americans, whether or not they committed the preponderance of crimes, would not be tolerated. As one black officer bluntly told journalist Tamar Jacoby: "I wouldn't write tickets for black kids."[32]

In 1976, Young cut the Detroit police force by 20% as a means of addressing the city's budget deficit, and Detroit became one of the most violent cities in the United States.[33] By 1987, the city's homicide rate was 3 times higher than it had been two decades earlier.[34] But when local residents complained about runaway crime, the mayor sneered that their calls for "law and order" were nothing more than "code" for "Keep the ni**ers in their place."[35]

Young further debased Detroit law-enforcement by putting his own corrupt people in charge. He appointed as police chief his close friend William Hart,[36] who in 1992 was convicted of embezzling $1.3 million from a police undercover anti-drug fund—money which he then lavished on female paramours while lying repeatedly to cover up his crimes.[37] Hart was eventually sentenced to 15 years in

---

[32] http://online.wsj.com/news/articles/SB10001424127887324110404578625581152645480

[33] http://online.wsj.com/news/articles/SB10001424127887324110404578625581152645480

[34] http://tinyurl.com/k8e8vfz

[35] http://online.wsj.com/news/articles/SB10001424127887324110404578625581152645480

[36] http://www.cnn.com/US/9711/29/young.obit.pm/

[37] http://www.nytimes.com/1992/05/08/us/former-detroit-police-chief-convicted-of-embezzlement.html; http://www.apnewsarchive.com/1992/Prosecutor-Ex-Chief-s-$2-6-Million-Theft-Shows-How-Power-Corrupts/id-5ca60a54bd33a361740eb2a6c1f037c2

prison.[38]

For good measure, Young also appointed his business associate and former investment advisor Kenneth Weiner—who had no prior police experience—as Detroit's civilian deputy police chief.[39] While in that post, Weiner conspired with William Hart to illegally divert another $1.3 million to phony corporations that Weiner controlled.[40] For this, Weiner would be incarcerated for five years.[41] In yet another matter, Weiner was convicted of all 40 counts against him for his role in a pyramid scheme through which he and Coleman Young had duped investors out of millions of dollars.[42]

Corruption by Democratic Party politicians has remained a hallmark of Detroit politics ever since Young's tenure. Some lowlights:

- In 2006, former Detroit City Council member Alonzo Bates was convicted of having improperly put one of his relatives on the city payroll, a transgression for

---

[38] http://www.nationalbcc.org/news/beyond-the-rhetoric/1694-detroit-free-falls-as-its-leaders-are-in-denial

[39] http://articles.latimes.com/1990-04-20/news/mn-1412_1_south-african-gold-coins; http://articles.chicagotribune.com/1991-02-13/news/9101130805_1_coleman-young-appointees-teresa-blossom

[40] http://www.apnewsarchive.com/1992/Prosecutor-Ex-Chief-s-$2-6-Million-Theft-Shows-How-Power-Corrupts/id-5ca60a54bd33a361740eb2a6c1f037c2

[41] http://www.nationalbcc.org/news/beyond-the-rhetoric/1694-detroit-free-falls-as-its-leaders-are-in-denial

[42] http://www.nytimes.com/1991/01/16/us/ex-official-guilty-in-detroit-fraud.html

which he was sentenced to 33 months in prison.[43]
- In 2009, Detroit City Council member Monica Conyers, wife of U.S. House Rep. John Conyers (D-Michigan), pleaded guilty to federal bribery charges and went on to serve 27 months in a federal penitentiary.[44]
- In 2008, Detroit mayor Kwame Kilpatrick agreed to resign from his office and spend four months in jail for two obstruction-of-justice felony counts.[45]
- In 2010, Kilpatrick was sentenced to additional jail time for violating the terms of his probation related to the 2008 conviction.[46]
- In March 2013, Kilpatrick was found guilty of 24 offenses including fraud, racketeering and extortion.[47]
- In 2012, Detroit Police Chief Ralph Godbee Jr. retired when it became publicly known that he was sexually involved with a female officer in the department.[48]

---

[43] http://www.frontpagemag.com/2013/arnold-ahlert/toxic-government-by-democrats-detroit-2/; http://www.freep.com/article/20130311/NEWS0102/130311042/Elected-leaders-their-legal-issues

[44] http://www.frontpagemag.com/2013/arnold-ahlert/toxic-government-by-democrats-detroit-2/

[45] http://www.frontpagemag.com/2013/arnold-ahlert/toxic-government-by-democrats-detroit-2/;

[46] http://www.foxnews.com/politics/2010/05/25/judge-sentences-detroit-mayor-kwame-kilpatrick-years-prison/

[47] http://www.frontpagemag.com/2013/arnold-ahlert/toxic-government-by-democrats-detroit-2/; http://www.nytimes.com/2013/03/12/us/kwame-kilpatrick-ex-mayor-of-detroit-convicted-in-corruption-case.html?_r=0&gwh=C9121B44C5BA0D101AFE9BA29981FFB8&gwt=pay

[48] http://www.frontpagemag.com/2013/arnold-ahlert/toxic-government-by-democrats-detroit-2/; http://www.freep.com/article/20121008/NEWS01/121008028

- In 2013, two Detroit city officials—pension-fund lawyer Ronald Zajac and Police & Fire pension trustee Paul Stewart—were indicted in a bribery scandal.[49]

Under the unbroken chain of Democrats who have led the city ever since 1961, Detroit has taken on some of the characteristics of an experiment in how to create a social underclass. Its population today is 82.7% black and 10.6% white,[50] a generation of racial hostility having destroyed what was once a racially balanced population. Under this new regime, traditional nuclear families, once the norm in Detroit's black community, are now a rarity. The city's out-of-wedlock birth rate exceeds 75%, and married-parent families with children younger than 18 constitute only 9.2% of all residents.[51]

Ruled by a series of black mayors, the Motor City's economic catastrophe is now both widespread and profound. Indeed, the population of Detroit has a per capita income of just $14,861 (scarcely half the national average), a median household income of $26,955 (about half the national median), and a poverty rate of 38.1% (about 2.5 times the U.S. average).[52] Since 1970, the number of Detroiters with

---

[49] http://www.frontpagemag.com/2013/arnold-ahlert/toxic-government-by-democrats-detroit-2/;

[50] http://quickfacts.census.gov/qfd/states/26/2622000.html

[51] http://www.frontpagemag.com/2013/arnold-ahlert/toxic-government-by-democrats-detroit-2/

[52] http://quickfacts.census.gov/qfd/states/26/2622000.html; http://quickfacts.census.gov/qfd/states/00000.html

jobs has dropped by more than 53%.[53]

Detroit's economic malaise has been brought about by decades of Democratic governance and practices that sociologist Thomas Sowell has termed the "Detroit Pattern," a reference to "increasing taxes, harassing businesses, and pandering to unions."[54] In any analysis of Detroit's tragic decline, these three factors bear close examination:

(1) Taxes:

Because of the middle-class population exodus caused by policies that inflamed race relations, Detroit's tax base has been in free fall, leading city leaders from the 1960s onward to try repeatedly to regain lost revenue through tax increases.[55] Today, Detroit's property-tax rates are the highest in America and generally twice as high as the overall average nationwide,[56] establishing a vicious cycle that continues to drive businesses away and cause taxpayers to relocate to the suburbs in still-larger numbers. By 2012, Detroit's tax *revenues*—notwithstanding the high *rates*—were 40% lower, in constant 2012 dollars, than they had been in 1962.[57]

[53] http://www.usatoday.com/story/money/personalfinance/2013/12/02/19-facts-about-detroit-bankruptcy/3823355/

[54] http://townhall.com/columnists/thomassowell/2011/03/22/obama_adminstration_is_following_the_detroit_pattern/page/full

[55] http://www.freep.com/interactive/article/20130915/NEWS01/130801004/Detroit-Bankruptcy-history-1950-debt-pension-revenue

[56] http://finance.townhall.com/columnists/chrisedwards/2013/07/29/detroits-high-property-taxes-n1651149

[57] http://www.freep.com/interactive/article/20130915/NEWS01/130801004/Detroit-Bankruptcy-history-1950-debt-pension-revenue

Another reason why Detroit's stratospheric tax rates have resulted in meager government revenues is because of the city's rapidly declining property values. Over the past half-century, the total assessed value of property in Detroit has fallen (in inflation-adjusted dollars) by 77%.[58] The median home price in Motown is now just $40,000, and many dwellings in the city's most blighted areas sell for less than $1,000.[59]

The non-payment of property taxes has also become a widespread phenomenon in Detroit. In 2012, for example, some 47% of all homeowners in the city elected not to pay their taxes—mainly because the city's cash-strapped government had failed to provide most of the basic services normally funded by such revenues.[60]

(2) Harassing Businesses:

In recent decades, the Democrats in control of Detroit have cultivated an oppressive climate for small businesses by instituting a complex constellation of protectionist regulations.[61] In 2013, economist Dean Stansel conducted

---

[58] http://www.usatoday.com/story/money/personalfinance/2013/12/02/19-facts-about-detroit-bankruptcy/3823355/

[59] http://www.forbes.com/sites/kurtbadenhausen/2013/02/21/detroit-tops-2013-list-of-americas-most-miserable-cities/; http://www.newgeography.com/content/003897-root-causes-detroit-s-decline-should-not-go-ignored

[60] http://www.detroitnews.com/article/20130221/METRO01/302210375; http://www.frontpagemag.com/2013/arnold-ahlert/how-the-democrats-destroyed-detroit/

[61] http://www.newgeography.com/content/003897-root-causes-detroit-s-decline-should-not-go-ignored

an "economic freedom" study that ranked the regulatory and tax climates of 384 U.S. metro areas, and found that Detroit placed 345th.[62] The Institute For Justice (IFJ) observes that the massive amounts of "time and money" that business owners must expend in order to comply with "all the regulatory requirements" of Detroit's "stupefying bureaucracy" cause many aspiring entrepreneurs to "simply give up their business dreams."[63]

Adds IFJ:

> "Multiple inspections and inspection fees, incomprehensible building requirements, expensive, mandatory public hearings, arbitrary discretion by officials, and lengthy processing delays combine to discourage entrepreneurs from undertaking business ventures or improving existing ones. From sign taxes to restrictions on planting trees, the bureaucratic shuffle has gotten so out of hand that one business owner explained, 'We operate on the basis that we just do what we want to do and the permits will catch up with us sometime.'"[64]

According to one survey, 56% of small-business owners in Detroit are unsure whether they are operating in full compliance with the law.[65]

---

[62] http://www.jrap-journal.org/pastvolumes/2010/v43/v43_n1_a2_stansel.pdf

[63] http://ij.org/detroit

[64] http://ij.org/detroit

[65] http://ippsr.msu.edu/policy/13MayPolicyBrief.pdf

(3) Pandering to Unions:

Detroit's network of nearly incomprehensible business regulations is largely the creation of its vast public bureaucracy, which is dominated by approximately four-dozen labor unions. Over time, the long succession of Democratic political administrations that have run Detroit have lavished such high salaries and lucrative pensions and health-benefit packages on members of these unions (whom they regard as their core political constituency), that it is now virtually impossible for the city to balance its budget and meet its financial obligations.[66] One of the consequences of this unholy alliance between Democratic politicians and union bosses is that current employee contributions can't keep pace with the needs of current pension recipients.

Today, Detroit's government sends monthly checks (with an average value of $1,600 apiece) to some 21,000 public-sector retirees and their families. This is more than twice the number of workers (9,700) who are currently employed by the city.[67] The pension obligations that Detroit owes to its retirees account for about half of the city's $18-to-$20 billion in long-term unfunded debt.[68]

---

[66] http://www.frontpagemag.com/2013/arnold-ahlert/how-the-democrats-destroyed-detroit/

[67] http://www.washingtonpost.com/blogs/wonkblog/wp/2013/07/19/detroits-pension-problems-in-one-chart/; http://www.usatoday.com/story/money/personalfinance/2013/12/02/19-facts-about-detroit-bankruptcy/3823355/

[68] http://blog.heritage.org/2013/07/22/detroit-and-the-bankruptcy-of-liberalism/; http://www.usatoday.com/story/money/personalfinance/2013/12/02/19-facts-about-detroit-bankruptcy/3823355/

By early 2013, Detroit's finances had become so chaotic that Michigan Governor Rick Snyder appointed attorney Kevyn Orr to serve as the city's emergency financial manager in a last-resort effort to avoid the largest municipal bankruptcy in American history. According to the *New York Times*, Orr was authorized "to cut city spending, change contracts with labor unions, merge or eliminate city departments, urge the sale of city assets and even, if all else fail[s], recommend bankruptcy proceedings."[69] Orr attributed Detroit's "dysfunctional and wasteful" operations to "years of budgetary restrictions, mismanagement, crippling operational practices and, in some cases, indifference or corruption."[70] In May 2013, he issued a report stating that the city was "clearly insolvent on a cash flow basis,"[71] that its budget deficit was approaching $386 million,[72] and that fully one-third of its budget was being spent on retiree benefits for former public-sector employees.[73] It was clear that without judicious and substantial cuts to retiree benefits, there would be no stopping this runaway fiscal train. But in July 2013, Detroit's two largest municipal pension funds filed suit in

---

[69] http://www.nytimes.com/2013/03/02/us/michigan-appoints-emergency-manager-for-detroit.html?hp&_r=0&gwh=62AECD70ABA2A0FBD24C1D41934CDC29&gwt=pay

[70] http://www.foxnews.com/politics/2013/05/13/report-by-emergency-manager-says-detroit-finances-are-crumbling-and-future-is/

[71] http://www.bbc.com/news/business-22514588

[72] http://www.foxnews.com/politics/2013/05/13/report-by-emergency-manager-says-detroit-finances-are-crumbling-and-future-is/

[73] http://www.usatoday.com/story/money/business/2013/05/13/detroit-emergency-financial-manager-report/2155081/

state court specifically to prevent Orr from instituting such cuts. Thus the city went ahead and filed for Chapter 9 bankruptcy.[74]

Another major financial drain on taxpayers has been the money that the city spends on its Detroit Public School (DPS) system—more than $15,500 per pupil, or nearly 50% more than the national average.[75] Notwithstanding these enormous outlays, U.S. Education Secretary Arne Duncan characterized DPS as a "national disgrace" in 2009.[76]

That same year, DPS was put under the control of an emergency financial manager—the Washington, DC Board of Education's former president, Robert Bobb—in an attempt to prevent bankruptcy. Bobb found that many of DPS's financial problems stemmed from willful corruption.[77] For instance:

- In June 2009, Bobb enlisted the services of a team of forensic accounting analysts who discovered that 257 "ghost" employees were illegally receiving paychecks from DPS.
- Two months later, seven additional public officials

---

[74] http://www.usatoday.com/story/news/nation/2013/07/18/detroit-prepares-bankruptcy-filing-friday/2552819/

[75] http://www.frontpagemag.com/2013/arnold-ahlert/detroit-public-schools-bankrupting-minority-students-futures/; http://detroit2020.com/2011/06/21/comparing-school-district-spending/

[76] http://online.wsj.com/news/articles/SB124813472753066949?mg=reno64-wsj&url=http%3A%2F%2Fonline.wsj.com%2Farticle%2FSB124813472753066949.html

[77] http://www.frontpagemag.com/2013/arnold-ahlert/toxic-government-by-democrats-detroit-2/; http://www.frontpagemag.com/2013/arnold-ahlert/detroit-public-schools-bankrupting-minority-students-futures/

were charged with felonies for operating an embezzlement scheme that siphoned tens of thousands of dollars out of the school system.[78]
- It was also discovered that some 500 people who had been illegally enrolled as healthcare-plan dependents were costing the school district millions of dollars per year.
- In 2012, a DPS contract accountant and her daughter, who was a schoolteacher, were indicted by the FBI on charges of fraud, conspiracy, and tax offenses.[79]

The appointment of DPS's emergency manager did nothing to improve student performance. In the National Assessment of Educational Progress, a U.S. Department of Education standardized test, fourth- and eighth-graders in the city's public schools currently read at a level that is 73% below the national average, and lower than that of students in any other urban school district in the country.[80] Similarly, the reading skills of Detroit's eighth-graders are 60% below the national average, and their math scores in 2009 were the lowest ever recorded in the then-40-year history of the exam.[81]

The results of exams that the Michigan Educational Assessment Program administered in 2012-13 to measure

---

[78] http://www.judicialwatch.org/blog/2009/08/more-corruption-detroit/

[79] http://www.fbi.gov/detroit/press-releases/2012/former-detroit-public-schools-accountant-teacher-indicted-on-fraud-and-money-laundering-charges

[80] http://www.mlive.com/news/detroit/index.ssf/2010/05/nations_report_card_detroit_st.html

[81] http://www.mlive.com/news/detroit/index.ssf/2009/12/detroit_students_notch_lowest.html

students' abilities in a variety of different subject areas provide further evidence of DPS's failed track record:

- The percentage of students whose scores indicated proficiency in math were: 15.7% of third-graders; 18.8% of fourth-graders; 17% of fifth-graders; 13.6% of sixth-graders; 13.2% of seventh-graders; and fewer than 11.1% of eighth-graders.
- The percentage of students whose scores indicated proficiency in reading were: 42.7% of third-graders; 40.7% of fourth-graders; 44.5% of fifth-graders; 45.3% of sixth-graders; 33% of seventh-graders; and 45.8% of eighth-graders.
- Only fifth- and eighth-graders were tested in science, and fewer than 10% of each group registered scores that indicated proficiency.
- Only sixth- and ninth-graders were tested in social studies, and fewer than 10% of each group registered scores that indicated proficiency.
- Only fourth- and seventh-graders were tested in writing, and just 19.5% of the former and 28% of the latter registered scores that indicated proficiency.[82]

In 1927, *New Republic* described the Detroit school system as "one of the finest in the world."[83] Today, it is one of the worst in the country. It is little wonder that a

---

[82] https://www.mischooldata.org/DistrictSchoolProfiles/AssessmentResults/Meap/MeapPerformanceSummary.aspx

[83] http://books.google.com/books?id=5ceGeWusD7gC&pg=PA217&source=gbs_toc_r&cad=3#v=onepage&q&f=false

recent survey of Detroit-area parents found that 79% of respondents did not want their children educated by the city's public schools.[84]

Apart from its catastrophic fiscal and educational problems, Detroit has long ranked as one of the most dangerous places in the United States.[85] Each year from 2009 through 2013, for instance, *Forbes* magazine rated Detroit as America's Most Dangerous City.[86] FBI data confirm that Detroit's metro division has the highest violent-crime rate in the nation.[87] Indeed, the city's homicide rate is now at its highest level in 40 years, and is more than 10 times greater than the national average.[88] In addition, the robbery rate in Detroit is about 6.1 times the national average; the assault rate is 5.5 times the national average; and property crimes like burglary and auto theft occur at rates that are 3 and 7 times higher, respectively, than the national average.[89]

The crime rates that plague Detroit are exacerbated by the fact that the city's financial woes have necessitated

---

[84] http://www.detroitnews.com/article/20121011/METRO01/210110335/1409/metro/Detroit-parents-embrace-school-choice-poll-says

[85] http://www.usatoday.com/story/money/personalfinance/2013/12/02/19-facts-about-detroit-bankruptcy/3823355/

[86] http://www.forbes.com/sites/danielfisher/2013/10/22/detroit-again-tops-list-of-most-dangerous-cities-but-crime-rate-dips/

[87] http://www.forbes.com/sites/kurtbadenhausen/2013/02/21/detroit-tops-2013-list-of-americas-most-miserable-cities/

[88] http://www.usatoday.com/story/money/personalfinance/2013/12/02/19-facts-about-detroit-bankruptcy/3823355/; http://www.forbes.com/sites/danielfisher/2013/10/22/detroit-again-tops-list-of-most-dangerous-cities-but-crime-rate-dips/

[89] http://www.city-data.com/crime/crime-Detroit-Michigan.html

budget (and manpower) cuts to the local police force. Thus, when Detroit residents place a phone call seeking help from the city's understaffed police department, they must wait an average of 58 minutes for an officer to arrive on the scene (vs. a national average of 11 minutes).[90]

Given this brief profile of steep urban decline, it is hardly surprising that a 2013 *Forbes* magazine analysis named Detroit as America's "most miserable" city.[91] Signs of this misery are everywhere visible in the city's blighted landscape. For example, Detroit has been the site of 11,000 to 12,000 fires every year for the past decade; it currently has just 370 functioning street lights per square mile, compared to 812 for Cleveland and 785 for St. Louis; more than half of its parks have been closed down since 2008; and it has approximately 99,000 vacant housing units (out of a total of 363,000).[92]

As far as Detroit has fallen, the city's future appears even bleaker than its present. The Democratic Party and the cadre of corrupt politicians it has empowered over the past fifty years have driven millions from this once-thriving metropolis and have left the remaining, largely black population to suffer in its ruins with little chance of escape. Yet they haven't stopped thinking about it; a 2012

---

[90] http://www.usatoday.com/story/money/personalfinance/2013/12/02/19-facts-about-detroit-bankruptcy/3823355/

[91] http://www.forbes.com/sites/kurtbadenhausen/2013/02/21/detroit-tops-2013-list-of-americas-most-miserable-cities/

[92] http://www.usatoday.com/story/money/personalfinance/2013/12/02/19-facts-about-detroit-bankruptcy/3823355/; http://www.frontpagemag.com/2013/arnold-ahlert/toxic-government-by-democrats-detroit-2/

Detroit News poll found that 40% of the city's residents hoped to leave Detroit within five years.[93]

Baltimore

In the 1950s and early '60s, Baltimore was booming. Known for its thriving industries—particularly manufacturing and shipping—these large enterprises created some three-fourths of all the jobs held by people in its metropolitan region.[94] The city at that time had nearly a million residents, 23% of whom were black. The median family income was 7% higher than the national average; the percentage of Baltimore families earning middle-class wages was about one-fifth higher than in the U.S. as a whole; and the proportion of Baltimoreans living in poverty was roughly one-fifth lower than the corresponding national figure.[95]

In 1967, however, this prosperity began to vanish when the city government was taken over by a string of Democratic mayors, persisting into the present day, who have made Baltimore into the grim and dangerous urban environment portrayed so chillingly in the television series *The Wire*. As in the case of other big cities around the country, while the Democratic Party machine was taking

---

[93] http://www.detroitnews.com/article/20121009/METRO01/210090369

[94] http://www.nathanielturner.com/robertmooreand1199union3.htm

[95] http://online.wsj.com/news/articles/SB10001424053111903480904576510794280560566; http://www.cato.org/publications/commentary/blame-taxes-baltimores-rot

control of the ballot box, the people were voting with their feet by leaving the city. Today Baltimore's population has declined to 622,000, 64% of it black.[96]

William Donald Schaefer, Baltimore's mayor from 1971-87, set the stage for economic decline in his city by championing an ever-expanding public sector as well as extensive government regulation of private business.[97] Further, he relied heavily on federal grants and city bonds to finance a host of development projects throughout Baltimore. As the *City Journal* reports: "[W]hen those monies proved insufficient, [Schaefer] ... created his own city bank to seed development: the Loan and Guarantee Fund. The fund financed itself by selling city property and then leasing it back to itself, and by selling bonds that would stick future taxpayers with much of the bill."[98]

Along with fiscal improvidence, Schaefer's administration was replete with the corruption and cronyism that has become the hallmark of the Democrats' big-city political machines over the last generation. For instance:

- The mayor's finance director, Charles Benton, once steered $5.6 million in public money to a repair project on an apartment building owned by a Schaefer political supporter.[99]

---

[96] http://quickfacts.census.gov/qfd/states/24/24510.html;

[97] http://msa.maryland.gov/msa/speccol/sc3500/sc3520/001400/001489/html/msa01489.html

[98] http://www.city-journal.org/html/11_1_can_mayor_omalley.html

[99] http://citypaper.com/news/saint-or-sinner-1.1144574

- On another occasion, Benton directed more than $4 million in taxpayer funds to the refurbishing of a hotel owned by a longtime friend of the mayor. The hotel went bankrupt shortly after Schaefer's mayoral tenure ended.[100]
- In the 1970s, Schaefer's deputy public works director was incarcerated for rigging bids on city contracts.[101]
- In the '80s, the federal government shut down Baltimore's Urban Development Action Grants program due to its many abuses.[102]

In 1987, Schaefer was succeeded by Baltimore's first elected black mayor, Kurt Schmoke, who, during his 12 years in office, continued his white predecessor's policy of extracting as much taxpayer money as possible from Annapolis and Washington. By 2001, such state and federal subsidies accounted for 40% of Baltimore's operating budget.[103]

Schmoke was a close friend of President Bill Clinton and had connections to a number of Clinton administration officials—most notably the disgraced Henry Cisneros and Andrew Cuomo, both heads of the Department of Housing & Urban Development (HUD)—ensuring that Baltimore's city programs would continue to receive high levels of

---

[100] http://citypaper.com/news/saint-or-sinner-1.1144574

[101] http://www.city-journal.org/html/11_1_can_mayor_omalley.html

[102] http://www.city-journal.org/html/11_1_can_mayor_omalley.html

[103] http://www.city-journal.org/html/11_1_can_mayor_omalley.html

federal support.[104] One such initiative—bankrolled by a ten-year, $100 million federal grant—was the establishment of an Empowerment Zone whose goal was to transform "distressed" areas of the city into "neighborhoods of choice" by implementing a host of job-training, workforce-development, home-construction, and drug-treatment programs.[105] All told, Baltimore's Empowerment Zone (EZ) covered nearly 10% of the city's total area.[106]

The results of this endeavor, though, were largely disappointing. As the *Baltimore Sun* reported in 2002, "the areas that make up the city's federally funded empowerment zone remain deeply troubled." Some specifics:

- The poverty rate within the EZ had dropped slightly (from 41.9% to 35.6%), but was still about 50% higher than the corresponding rate citywide.
- Median household income had risen in slightly more than half of the EZ area, but had declined in the rest and was below the citywide median in 92% of the EZ area.
- Homeownership rates in the EZ had increased modestly, from 30% to 35%—but not nearly as much as officials had predicted; moreover,

---

[104] http://www2.citypaper.com/news/story.asp?id=3501; http://baltimore.indymedia.org/newswire/display/2416/index.php

[105] http://www.ubalt.edu/jfi/jfi/reports/EBMCJobCreation0905.pdf; http://www.highbeam.com/doc/1P1-2240408.html; http://carnegie.org/about-us/board-of-directors/kurt-l-schmoke/; http://articles.baltimoresun.com/2002-11-05/news/0211050405_1_empowerment-basu-census;

[106] http://articles.baltimoresun.com/2002-11-05/news/0211050405_1_empowerment-basu-census

homeownership in the EZ was still 15 percentage points lower than the citywide rate.
- Unemployment in the EZ had increased from 14.9% to 16.5%, and was about 50% higher than Baltimore's overall rate.
- And perhaps most tellingly, the EZ region had lost population at more than double the rate of the city as a whole.[107]

Like Schaefer's, the Schmoke administration was scarred by corruption. In the mid-1990s, for instance, federal officials were alerted to the fact that the mayor's Housing Authority had squandered—via no-bid contracts, massive cost overruns, and blatant cronyism—some $25.6 million in Department of Housing & Urban Development (HUD) funds that had been earmarked for housing repairs. Ultimately, the scandal resulted in federal convictions against 13 contractors.[108]

For awhile it appeared that even Schmoke himself might find his political career in jeopardy when, in 1998, HUD's inspector general announced a probe of the mayor's handling of federal housing aid. However, both Schmoke and his housing chief, Dan Henson, were able to disarm investigators by playing the race card. At their instigation, West Baltimore black Congressman Elijah Cummings demanded that the White House launch a special

---

[107] http://baltimore.indymedia.org/newswire/display/2416/index.php; http://articles.baltimoresun.com/2002-11-05/news/0211050405_1_empowerment-basu-census

[108] http://www.city-journal.org/html/11_1_can_mayor_omalley.html

investigation into the inspector general's investigation. In the end, Schmoke escaped unscathed when HUD Secretary Andrew Cuomo quashed the probe.[109]

America as a whole may have flourished in the 1990s, but Baltimore's economy foundered under Democrats' stewardship. Contributing to this state of affairs was the fact that in the preceding decades, Baltimore's property taxes, the highest in all of Maryland, had been repeatedly raised. Businesses, in turn, voted with their feet and many of the city's leading private-sector firms, in search of a more business-friendly climate, relocated to the suburbs during the Nineties. Thus, between 1990 and 1999, Baltimore lost some 58,000 jobs. These included approximately 13,000 in the manufacturing sector; another 12,300 in the finance, insurance, and real-estate industries; and 23,400 in retail and wholesale businesses. During the worst of times on Mayor Schmoke's watch, Baltimore's overall work force shrank by an average of 722 people *per month*. The city's unemployment rate during the '90s was twice that of the rest of Maryland.[110]

While Baltimore's industry and finance were in steep decline, crime was on the rise—thanks, in large measure, to Schmoke's decision to focus the city's policing strategy on decriminalizing drugs rather than on tackling violent crime. As a result, by the end of the 1990s, the murder

---

[109] http://www.city-journal.org/html/11_1_can_mayor_omalley.html; http://www2.citypaper.com/news/story.asp?id=3501

[110] http://online.wsj.com/news/articles/SB20001424053111903480904576510794280560566; http://www.city-journal.org/html/11_1_can_mayor_omalley.html

rate in Baltimore was six times higher than in New York[111] (where a variety of proactive policing practices instituted by mayor Rudy Guiliani had dramatically reduced serious crime.)[112] Throughout the Nineties, Baltimore was the scene of more than 300 murders every year, prompting locals to nickname their city—which had become the second-deadliest in the nation—"Bodymore, Murderland." Approximately 75% of Baltimore's killings were drug-related—symptoms of an ongoing, brutal drug-turf war that was allowed to engulf many black neighborhoods. Police, meanwhile, were frustrated by the fact that those drug dealers they arrested were routinely released a short time later, as a result of Schmoke's "philosophy," free to resume their criminal activities on the streets. One police sergeant lamented that under Schmoke's leadership, Baltimore had become a city "in love with its own victimhood."[113]

The casual attitude on the part of Baltimore's leadership toward drug crimes may have pleased the city's liberal elites, but it devastated the minority community, whose champion it otherwise pretended to be. As of 2000, only 23 detectives in the entire city were actively investigating narcotics cases—even while epidemics of heroin and cocaine abuse, particularly among black males, reached levels unmatched in virtually any other American city. Further, just four officers in all of Baltimore were tasked with tracking down the suspects who had been named in

---

[111] http://www.city-journal.org/html/11_1_can_mayor_omalley.html

[112] http://www.discoverthenetworks.org/viewSubCategory.asp?id=1633; http://www.discoverthenetworks.org/viewSubCategory.asp?id=1629

[113] http://www.city-journal.org/html/11_1_can_mayor_omalley.html

some 54,000 open arrest warrants—250 of them for murder or attempted murder.[114]

Baltimore's widespread political corruption, failing economy, high taxes, and escalating crime rates, caused its population to fall by more than 120,000 during the 1990s, making the city blacker and poorer.[115] Tens of thousands of homes were simply abandoned by residents desperate to leave town.

In 1999, Democratic city councilman Martin O'Malley won Baltimore's mayoral race by campaigning on a law-and-order platform, but in part because of the legacy he inherited, he was ultimately unable to fulfill his crime-reduction pledges. In 2005, when his tenure was nearing its end, criminal-justice statistics for Baltimore indicated that 17.6 violent crimes were committed for every 1,000 residents—a figure almost 80% higher than America's big-city average. Baltimore's murder rate, meanwhile, was nearly three times higher than the big-city average—just as it had been when O'Malley first took office in 2000. Robberies and aggravated assaults (including nonfatal shootings) had dropped slightly since 2000, but were still more than twice as prevalent as in other large American cities.[116]

Meanwhile, Baltimore's anemic economy lagged even further under O'Malley's stewardship. Between 2001 and

---

[114] http://www.city-journal.org/html/11_1_can_mayor_omalley.html
[115] http://www.city-journal.org/html/11_1_can_mayor_omalley.html
[116] http://www2.citypaper.com/news/story.asp?id=12855

2004, the city lost nearly 5% of all its remaining jobs, including a quarter of its manufacturing jobs, 15% of its banking and finance jobs, and 5% of its retail jobs.[117] From 2000 to 2007, private-sector employment in Baltimore shrank by 10.4%—a loss of approximately 33,600 jobs. During that same seven-year period, employment in the areas immediately *outside* of Baltimore grew by 13.9%—after having grown by 25.1% during the 1990s.[118]

In 2007, O'Malley was succeeded as mayor by fellow Democrat Sheila Dixon, who was forced to resign three years later when convicted of embezzlement and perjury.[119] Replacing Dixon was another black Democrat, city council president Stephanie Rawlings-Blake.

Today, Baltimore's residents have a median household income of $38,721 (about 45% below Maryland's state average) and a poverty rate of 25.1% (about 1.7 times the national average).[120] Among America's 100 most populous cities, Baltimore ranks 87th in median household income.[121]

The violent crime rate in Baltimore is currently 3.7 times higher than the national average. This figure includes astronomical rates of murder (6.6 times the national

---

[117] http://www2.citypaper.com/news/story.asp?id=12855

[118] http://www.cato.org/publications/commentary/blame-taxes-baltimores-rot

[119] http://articles.baltimoresun.com/2010-02-04/news/bal-dixon-sentenced0204_1_ronald-h-lipscomb-plea-deal-perjury

[120] http://www.city-data.com/city/Baltimore-Maryland.html

[121] http://www.cato.org/publications/commentary/blame-taxes-baltimores-rot

average), rape (twice the national average), robbery (4.8 times the national average), and assault (3.2 times the national average).[122]

Once Baltimore's public schools were racially balanced; today 84% of the students are black and another 6% are Hispanic.[123] Baltimore's Democratic leaders claim to be looking out for the welfare of the city's minorities, yet find its minority students easy to ignore.

Funding is not a problem. The Baltimore City Public Schools (BCPS) spend, on average, $15,483 for each K-12 student in their jurisdiction—almost 50% more than the national average.[124] But achievement is paltry. Baltimore's students perform near the bottom on the National Assessment of Educational Progress (NAEP), a standardized test that measures the academic abilities of children in elementary and junior high school. In 2013, for example, NAEP results indicated that only 14% of Baltimore's fourth-graders, and 16% of its eighth-graders, were able to read proficiently. In math, the corresponding proficiency figures for fourth- and eighth-graders were 19% and 13%.[125]

Notwithstanding this abysmal track record, the

---

[122] http://www.city-data.com/crime/crime-Baltimore-Maryland.html

[123] http://www.bpichicago.org/wp-content/uploads/2014/03/Beshon+Smith+presentation.pdf

[124] https://www.census.gov/newsroom/releases/archives/governments/cb13-92.html; http://nces.ed.gov/fastfacts/display.asp?id=66

[125] http://articles.baltimoresun.com/2013-12-18/news/bs-md-ci-tuda-results-20131218_1_common-core-trial-urban-district-assessment-average-reading-scores

Baltimore Teachers Union (BTU), which is a reliable bulwark for Democratic Party causes and candidates in the city, has successfully opposed any calls for a voucher program that would enable low-income parents to take their children out of the city's failing public schools and send them instead—for a fraction of the cost—to a private or parochial school.[126] And of course Baltimore Democrats, knowing that a substantial portion of BTU union dues are funneled directly into their party's coffers, likewise abjure voucher proposals—just as Democrats have done in city after city across the United States. Joel Klein, former chancellor of the New York City Department of Education, once explained candidly: "[P]oliticians—especially Democratic politicians—generally do what the unions want. And the unions, in turn, are very clear about what that is. They want, first, happy members, so that those who run the unions get reelected; and, second, more members, so their power, money, and influence grow."[127]

This educational train wreck is largely funded by Baltimore's stratospheric property taxes, twice as high as those of any other jurisdiction in Maryland or the District of Columbia.[128] The city's residents have become accustomed not only to high taxation, but to the use of taxes as a weapon in a war of divide-and-conquer. As economists Steve Hanke

---

[126] http://www.baltimorecityschools.org/cms/lib/MD01001351/Centricity/Domain/8861/PDF/2014-LegislativePlatform.pdf

[127] http://www.theatlantic.com/magazine/archive/2011/06/the-failure-of-american-schools/308497/?single_page=true

[128] http://online.wsj.com/news/articles/SB10001424053111903480904576510794280560566

of Johns Hopkins University and Stephen Walters of Loyola University write: "In modern Baltimore, the [political] machine has exploited class divisions, not ethnic ones. Officials raised property taxes 21 times between 1950 and 1985 ... causing many homeowners and entrepreneurs—disproportionately Republicans—to flee."[129]

But just as high taxes have failed to buy a decent education for Baltimore's schoolchildren, so have they failed to cover the costs of runaway government spending under a long succession of fiscally irresponsible Democrats in high office. By December 2012, the unfunded pension liabilities that Baltimore owed to its retired police and firefighters had reached an unprecedented $765 million.[130]

As a result of Baltimore's multiple social, economic, and educational problems, some 47,000 abandoned houses and 16,000 vacant buildings now stand like pulled teeth in Baltimore's once vibrant but now depleted and depressed neighborhoods.[131]

---

[129] https://www.baltimorebrew.com/2011/08/27/are-high-property-taxes-"killing"-baltimore/

[130] http://www.baltimoresun.com/news/maryland/politics/blog/bal-city-police-and-fire-unfunded-pension-liabilities-grow-by-60m-20131216,0,430951.story

[131] http://online.wsj.com/news/articles/SB10001424053111903480904576510794280560566; http://www.theatlanticcities.com/design/2013/05/second-life-some-baltimores-vacant-lots/5764/

Washington, DC

Founded in 1790 and named after the first President, Washington, DC was established by the U.S. Constitution to serve as the seat of America's federal government.[132] Between 1800 and 1820, DC's population grew from about 5,000 to more than 13,200, making it the country's ninth largest city.[133] By 1840, that figure had mushroomed to 23,364, and two decades later it stood at 61,122.[134]

As a Southern city, DC, from its earliest days, always had a substantial African American population that included a growing number of free blacks who worked as craftsmen, hack drivers, businessmen and laborers. Slavery was abolished in the capital on April 16, 1862—about eight months before President Lincoln issued the Emancipation Proclamation.[135]

Beginning in 1871, DC was governed by a three-member Board of Commissioners, two of whom were appointed by the U.S. President after approval by the Senate, and a third who was selected from the U.S. Army Corps of Engineers. The city would retain this political arrangement for nearly a century, until 1967 when Congress passed a law

---

[132] http://washington.org/DC-information/washington-dc-history

[133] http://www.eyewitnesstohistory.com/capital.htm; http://www.census.gov/history/www/through_the_decades/fast_facts/1820_fast_facts.html

[134] http://www.census.gov/population/www/documentation/twps0027/tab07.txt; http://www.census.gov/population/www/documentation/twps0027/tab09.txt

[135] http://washington.org/DC-information/washington-dc-history

eliminating the three-commissioner form of government and replacing it with a single commissioner and a nine-member city council, all appointed by the President.

During the latter decades of the 19th century, DC continued to grow at a brisk pace; by 1900 its population had reached 278,718.[136] Many new roads were built in the city at that time, so as to extend, like an ever-expanding network, to its remotest reaches. And in 1900, Congress formed the Senate Park Improvement Commission which drew up an architectural plan for the redevelopment of the National Mall—with an eye toward emulating the grandeur of European capitals such as Paris, London, and Rome.

After World War II, Washington was a destination for large numbers of Southern blacks emigrating to Northern cities in pursuit of job opportunities. By 1957, DC had become the first major American city with a majority-black population.[137] Six years later, Washington took center stage in the American Civil Rights Movement when Martin Luther King Jr. delivered his historic "I Have a Dream" speech at the Lincoln Memorial.

Following King's assassination in Memphis in April 1968, DC was devastated by four days of race riots that resulted in 10 deaths, at least 1,200 fires, more than 7,600 arrests, and over $13 million in property damage. The violence had a profound effect on the people of DC, causing many whites, middle-class blacks, and business owners to

---
[136] http://www.census.gov/population/www/documentation/twps0027/tab13.txt
[137] http://www.city-journal.org/2013/23_1_washington-dc.html

flee the city and resettle elsewhere.[138]

In 1973, Congress passed the District of Columbia Home Rule Act, which for the first time placed the city under the governance of a directly elected mayor and a Council. The first elected mayor under this new arrangement was Walter Washington. And every DC mayor since then has been, like Mr. Washington, a Democrat.

Mayor Washington opposed the increasing tendency of his party to pit blacks and whites against one another for their own political advantage—"playing the race card," it would later be called. The *Washington Post* once quoted him as saying, "This city is already too much divided along race and income lines. We have got to take the lead and set the example in bringing this city together. We've got to become just one Washington." He was also an effective administrator; by the time he left office in 1978, DC's city government was running a $40 million yearly surplus.[139]

But Mayor Washington's successor, Marion Barry, was a master at racial division, and also incompetent and crooked. During his administration, the nation's capital became a center of scandal and something of a national joke.

In the 1970s, Barry, who had worked for the Student

---

[138] http://greatergreaterwashington.org/post/10005/43-years-ago-today-dc-stopped-burning/; http://www.mnn.com/lifestyle/responsible-living/stories/washington-dc-is-booming-but-racial-divide-causes-unease

[139] http://www.answers.com/topic/walter-washington

Nonviolent Coordinating Committee (SNCC) as a young man, served as president of the DC Board of Education and as a member of the DC Council.[140] He won his first mayoral race in 1978 and was subsequently reelected by wide margins in 1982 and 1986. "During his tenure in the 1980s," reports the *City Journal*, "unchecked corruption, ineptly delivered city services, soaring crime, horrendous public schools, financial chaos, and racial tensions made the city a byword for dysfunction nationally."[141] By the early 1990s, DC was the site of several hundred homicides per year and was dubbed the "murder capital" of the nation (a dubious honor that would rotate among almost all of the country's big cities in the years to come.)[142] The city's economy, meanwhile, was in shambles—notwithstanding the $400 million in federal aid it received each year.[143]

Throughout his years as mayor, Barry worked hard to expand the rolls of Washington's public employees. Indeed, even as the District's population fell by nearly 30,000 during Barry's three terms (1979-1991), the number of public-sector bureaucrats in the city increased by some 10,000.[144] By 1992, an astonishing 52,000 people—one in twelve city residents—were on DC's municipal payroll.

---

[140] http://www.washingtonpost.com/wp-srv/local/longterm/library/dc/barry/timeline.htm

[141] http://www.city-journal.org/2013/23_1_washington-dc.html

[142] http://articles.baltimoresun.com/1991-04-29/news/1991119021_1_crime-increased-violent-crime-capita

[143] http://articles.latimes.com/1990-01-07/news/mn-442_1_marion-barry/6

[144] http://www.nytimes.com/1990/07/12/us/two-worlds-of-washington-turmoil-and-growth.html?pagewanted=print; http://articles.latimes.com/1990-01-07/news/mn-442_1_marion-barry/6

Los Angeles—a city whose population was five times larger than DC's—had 14,000 fewer taxpayer-funded workers.[145]

Despite the massive number of public employees in DC, vital city services were hopelessly inefficient and chaotic. As a 1990 *Los Angeles Times* piece stated: "The city is under court order to correct prison and mental health facilities. Nearly half of all public housing sits idle for lack of repairs. Bureaucrats are so incompetent, arrogant and slothful, critics say, that even 9-1-1 calls go unanswered and ambulances may not arrive until tomorrow."[146] On seven separate occasions between 1987 and 1990, judges cited DC for the systematic mistreatment of juvenile delinquents, prison inmates, and mentally handicapped residents in its custody in specialized facilities.[147] In 1989, the *Washington Monthly* characterized Barry's administration as "the worst city government in America."[148] The mayor, unfazed by such assessments, routinely chalked them up to racism on the part of his critics.[149]

Barry's mayoralty was infamous not only for its gross incompetence but also for the magnitude of its corruption. One of his appointments that drew attention was that of

---

[145] http://archive.frontpagemag.com/readArticle.aspx?ARTID=36213

[146] http://articles.latimes.com/1990-01-07/news/mn-442_1_marion-barry/6

[147] http://connection.ebscohost.com/c/articles/9007301339/marion-barrys-untold-legacy

[148] http://www.thefreelibrary.com/The+worst+city+government.-a07371279; http://www.theatlantic.com/past/docs/issues/97may/kennedy2.htm

[149] http://articles.latimes.com/1990-01-07/news/mn-442_1_marion-barry/2

Ivanhoe Donaldson, his longtime friend and ally from SNCC, whom he appointed deputy mayor for economic development. In 1985, Donaldson pled guilty to stealing $190,000 from the city, and eventually wound up in prison for his crime. For good measure, Donaldson also obstructed justice by attempting to persuade four individuals to submit false affidavits to DC inspectors.[150]

After Barry's 1986 reelection, two more DC deputy mayors and ten additional city officials were charged with corruption.[151] One of these, deputy mayor for finance Alphonse G. Hill, was indicted on eleven counts of extortion, income tax evasion, and defrauding the District government—charges to which he eventually pled guilty.[152]

Standing behind the corruption was Barry himself and his personal problems. Throughout the '80s, rumors circulated about his frequent cocaine use. Though the evidence to that effect was highly credible, Barry for years managed to elude the grip of law-enforcement authorities—thanks, in large part, to friends and supporters who helped him stonewall investigations. One such ally, Karen K. Johnson, was paid $25,000 to keep silent regarding the cocaine allegations and was cited for contempt of court

---

[150] http://www.washingtonpost.com/wp-srv/local/longterm/library/dc/barry/87prof.htm; http://www.washingtonpost.com/wp-srv/local/longterm/library/dc/barry/timeline.htm; http://keywiki.org/index.php/Ivanhoe_Donaldson

[151]m http://books.google.com/books?id=EUVXKwkHuaQC&pg=PA12&lpg=PA12&dq=mayor+#v=onepage&q=mayor%20&f=false

[152] http://www.washingtonpost.com/wp-srv/local/longterm/library/dc/barry/timeline.htm

when she refused to testify before a federal grand jury that was probing the matter. The truth was finally revealed, however, in a January 18, 1990 sting operation, when Barry—lured to a Washington hotel room by a former girlfriend-turned-FBI-informant—was secretly filmed smoking a crack pipe.[153]

At his subsequent indictment, Barry once again raised the specter of race, lamenting that he was the victim of a "political lynching."[154] The charge of racism was picked up by civil rights professionals such as NAACP executive director Benjamin Hooks, who denounced Barry's prosecution as "Nazilike," charging that "overzealous, hostile—if not openly racist—district and U.S. attorneys will bring a black official to trial on the flimsiest of evidence."[155]

When Barry was tried for 14 counts of cocaine possession and lying to a grand jury, a jury of ten blacks and two whites convicted him of only a single cocaine-possession charge, for which he was sentenced to six months in prison.[156] Black columnist Carl Rowan put the

---

[153] http://www.washingtonpost.com/wp-srv/local/longterm/library/dc/barry/time-line.htm; http://www.wtop.com/41/2894587/A-timeline-of-DCs-troubled-political-past-; http://www.washingtonpost.com/wp-srv/local/longterm/library/dc/barry/video.htm

[154] http://news.google.com/newspapers?nid=1817&dat=19900215&id=CTsdAAAAIBAJ&sjid=IKYEAAAAIBAJ&pg=2734,3894746

[155] http://articles.baltimoresun.com/1994-05-20/news/1994140041_1_marion-barry-witness-barry-knew

[156] http://www.washingtonpost.com/wp-srv/local/longterm/library/dc/barry/time-line.htm; http://www.wtop.com/41/2894587/A-timeline-of-DCs-troubled-political-past-

Barry case in perspective: "These jurors were saying: The mayor may be a cocaine junkie, a crack addict, a sexual scoundrel, but he is *our* junkie, *our* addict, *our* scoundrel, and we aren't going to let you white folks put him in jail."[157]

Just two months after his release from prison in 1992, Barry—disgraced but not chastened—filed papers to run for DC's Ward 8 Council seat in that year's upcoming election. Campaigning under the slogan, "He May Not Be Perfect, But He's Perfect for DC," Barry won the race easily.[158] Two years after that, he decided to set his political sights higher and was elected to a fourth term (1995-99) as mayor.

After taking some time away from politics, Barry won election to the DC Council in 2004 with 95% of the vote and continues in that office.[159]

A mainstay of the Democratic Party, Marion Barry has been a larger-than-life figure in Washington DC politics in terms of his corruption, criminality and race-baiting. But those who followed him in city leadership have come close to matching his sordid record. Indeed, half of DC's top government officials, at one time or another, were under investigation by either federal authorities or the city's board of elections in the period 2008-2012.[160]

---

[157] http://www.newrepublic.com/article/113906/al-sharpton-after-trayvon-martin-end-racial-demagoguery

[158] http://www.nytimes.com/2009/08/10/arts/television/10barry.html?_r=0

[159] http://tinyurl.com/l6x5ph8

[160] http://abcnews.go.com/Politics/OTUS/dcs-delinquents-top-corrupt-politicians-washington/story?id=16520422

The following snapshots from recent DC politics give a sense of the corruption presided over by the Democratic Party, corruption that has become standard operating procedure:

- In October 2005, the *Washington Post* reported that DC Councilman Jack Evans had used money from a political action committee to cover personal expenses, including sporting-event tickets and a friend's trip to China.[161]
- In November 2007, Harriette Walters, manager of the DC Real Property Tax Administration Adjustments Unit, was one of 11 people arrested for her role in the largest fraud scheme in the history of DC's city government. As *The New York Times* reports, "Walters used her job as a tax manager for the district treasury to issue $48 million in bogus property tax refunds for herself and her co-conspirators, who included family, friends and a bank manager." The refunds—which amounted, on average, to $388,000 per month—were used to purchase such items as clothing, jewelry, other luxury goods, and even homes. Walters was sentenced to more than 17 years in prison for her crimes.[162]
- In January 2011, DC's newly elected mayor, Vince Gray, was accused of improperly hiring relatives of his supporters and staffers for city jobs.[163]

---

[161] http://www.wtop.com/41/2894587/A-timeline-of-DCs-troubled-political-past-; http://www.washingtoncitypaper.com/articles/45047/swagger-jack/

[162] http://www.wtop.com/41/2894587/A-timeline-of-DCs-troubled-political-past-; http://www.nytimes.com/2009/07/01/us/01embezzle.html

[163] http://www.wtop.com/41/2894587/A-timeline-of-DCs-troubled-political-past-

- In February 2011, while DC was facing a projected annual budget deficit of $400 million, it was learned that city taxpayers were making lease payments on two luxury automobiles—each in the amount of approximately $1,900 per month—for Council chairman Kwame Brown. Brown had initially requested a fully loaded, extended-wheelbase Lincoln Navigator with a black interior. When he instead received a Navigator with a gray interior, he defiantly ordered the second vehicle—and had the city pay an additional $1,500 for its expedited shipping.[164]
- In June 2011, a video surfaced of Ted Loza, former chief of staff to DC Councilman Jim Graham, accepting a $1,500 bribe from an FBI informant in return for pushing legislation that was beneficial to some in the taxi-cab industry through the DC Council. Loza was eventually sentenced to eight months in prison.[165]
- In July 2011, the DC Board of Elections and Ethics referred, to the U.S. Attorney's Office, allegations that DC Council chairman Kwame Brown's 2008 reelection campaign had failed to report more than $170,000 in contributions while inaccurately reporting almost $350,000 in spending. In 2012, Brown pled guilty to bank fraud and resigned from his post.[166]

---

[164] http://www.washingtonpost.com/wp-dyn/content/article/2011/02/19/AR2011021904613.html; http://www.wtop.com/41/2894587/A-timeline-of-DCs-troubled-political-past-;

[165] http://tinyurl.com/pyvmsrc

[166] http://tinyurl.com/pvsenj6

- In January 2012, Ward 5 councilman Harry Thomas Jr. pled guilty to the felony of embezzling some $353,000 in public funds that had been intended mostly for a youth baseball program. Thomas used the money instead to purchase for himself such items as designer shoes, a $58,000 luxury automobile, a $23,000 motorcycle, and lavish vacations. He was sentenced to 38 months in prison.[167]
- In June 2013, DC Council member Michael Brown pled guilty to accepting $55,000 in cash bribes from undercover agents posing as businessmen seeking city contracts.[168]
- In March 2014, businessman Jeffrey E. Thompson pled guilty to conspiring to break federal and local campaign-finance laws. At issue was more than $668,000 in illegal donations he had given to the Vince Gray mayoral campaign, with Gray's full knowledge. Moreover, Thompson had secretly spent $812,146 in support of seven other candidates for mayor and DC Council.[169]

In addition to becoming America's urban capital of political corruption, the District of Columbia has also become a synonym for criminality and violence. Though the city's crime rates today are below the stratospheric

---

[167] http://tinyurl.com/ms8xaa4

[168] http://www.washingtonpost.com/local/former-dc-council-member-michael-brown-expected-to-plead-guilty-to-bribe-charge-monday/2013/06/10/7bf75812-d1d5-11e2-8cbe-1bcbee06f8f8_story.html

[169] http://www.washingtonpost.com/local/crime/jeffrey-thompson-alleged-shadow-campaign-funder-is-charged-in-federal-court/2014/03/10/7bf6ca14-99a8-11e3-80-ac-63a8ba7f7942_story.html

levels which they reached during Marion Barry's heyday, DC remains an unsafe place by any measure. Today it is America's 5th most dangerous city among those with populations of more than 500,000, and the 21st most dangerous city overall.[170] Indeed, 95% of all urban areas in the U.S. are statistically safer than Washington,[171] whose rates of homicide and robbery are, respectively, 3 and 5 times higher than the national average.[172] In 2012 alone, there were 7,448 violent crimes and 29,264 property crimes reported in DC.[173]

Yet another major problem area for the nation's capital is its public school system. As bad as many of them are, no other system in America has a more glaring record of failure. When the National Assessment of Educational Progress tests were administered, most recently, to fourth- and eigth-grade students in 2013:

- Just 25% of DC fourth-graders performed well enough to be classified as "proficient" in grade-level reading.[174]
- Only 30% of DC fourth-graders performed well enough to be classified as "proficient" in grade-

---

[170] http://www.businessinsider.com/the-25-most-dangerous-cities-in-america-2012--10?op=1

[171] http://www.neighborhoodscout.com/dc/washington/crime/

[172] http://www.city-data.com/crime/crime-Washington-District-of-Columbia.html

[173] http://www.fbi.gov/about-us/cjis/ucr/crime-in-the.u.s/2012/crime-in-the.u.s.-2012/tables/8tabledatadecpdf/table-8-state-cuts/table_8_offenses_known_to_law_enforcement_by_district_of_columbia_by_city_2012.xls

[174] http://nccs.cd.gov/nationsreportcard/subject/publications/dst2013/pdf/2014467XW4.pdf

level math.[175]
- A paltry 17% of DC eighth-graders performed well enough to be categorized as "proficient" in grade-level reading.[176]
- And a mere 16% of DC eighth-graders performed well enough to be deemed "proficient" in grade-level math.[177]

When Adrian Fenty became mayor in 2007, the teacher-to-pupil ratio in Washington's public school classrooms was approximately 12-to-1, while taxpayers provided nearly $29,000 per year to educate each child therein. This massive sum was equivalent to the cost of tuition at the most elite private schools in the country, where children received the best education that money could buy.[178] A contrarian Democrat, Fenty tried to do something about this outrage. He hired Michelle Rhee, an education reformer, as the new school chancellor. He closed dangerous and underused schools and laid off incompetent teachers. He waged a successful two-year battle to get a new union contract, which ended lifetime tenure and connected financial reward to teacher performance. Michelle Rhee fired 241 incompetent teachers and put another 737 on

---

[175] http://nces.ed.gov/nationsreportcard/subject/publications/dst2013/pdf/2014468XW4.pdf

[176] http://nces.ed.gov/nationsreportcard/subject/publications/dst2013/pdf/2014467XW8.pdf

[177] http://nces.ed.gov/nationsreportcard/subject/publications/dst2013/pdf/2014468XW8.pdf

[178] http://blog.heritage.org/2012/07/25/d-c-public-schools-spend-almost-30000-per-student/

notice for being rated "minimally effective."[179]

The results were dramatic. At Sousa Middle School—located in one of the district's most impoverished neighborhoods—84% of the students had math and reading scores below the minimal standards when Fenty and Rhee took charge. In just one year of the Fenty-Rhee reform administration, students at Sousa gained 17 points in reading proficiency and 25 in math, meeting the federal benchmarks for progress for the first time in the history of the school.[180]

But the teachers' unions struck back in 2012, supporting another Democrat, Vincent Gray, who would turn back the clock on Fenty's reforms. The party backed Gray, and the head of the AFL-CIO himself came to town to campaign against Fenty and seal his defeat. In the process, he also sealed the fate of the many students, most of them black, who were stuck in the city's atrocious public schools.

---

[179] http://www.nytimes.com/2010/07/24/education/24teachers.html
[180] http://online.wsj.com/news/articles/SB10001424052702303362404575580221511231074

Chicago

Hog Butcher for the World,
Tool Maker, Stacker of Wheat,
Player with Railroads and the Nation's Freight Handler;
Stormy, husky, brawling ...

This is how Carl Sandberg saw Chicago in his famous poem about the city published in 1914.[181] He was right to use the language of enterprise and simple hard work, since the Windy City, standing at the crossroads of the United States, was so intimately associated with the nation-building epic. Chicago was the site of stockyards for the livestock that fed the country . It was the home of such technological and commercial innovations as the first refrigerated railroad car (1878), the first mail-order retailing corporations (Sears-Roebuck in 1893 and Montgomery Ward in 1872), and the first car radio manufacture (1920s).[182] Also during the Twenties, new construction boomed throughout the city, punctuated by the completion in 1930 of such landmarks as the Chicago Board of Trade Building and the famed Merchandise Mart (whose 4 million square feet of office space made it the world's largest building at the time). The fact that it was also the home turf of gangsters like Al Capone and the G-men like Elliot Ness who hunted him down only added to the legendary status it acquired in the nation's imagination.

---

[181] http://www.poetryfoundation.org/poetrymagazine/poem/2043

[182] http://www.cityofchicago.org/city/en/about/history.html; http://www.radiomuseum.org/forum/first_car_radios_history_and_development_of_early_car_radios.html

"Chicagoland," as the city is now sometimes called, is meant to conjure a zesty sense of urban uniqueness, but the term has instead become a synonym for corrupt power politics and urban malaise in what has become the murder capital of the United States. Chicago has been led exclusively by Democratic mayors since 1931. Under the administrations of Richard J. Daley (1955-76), Michael Bilandic (1976-79), Jane Byrne (1979-83), and Harold Washington (1983-87), the city's economic and social fabric deteriorated markedly. Chicago lost its power and romance.[183] According to urban analyst Aaron Renn, by 1976 Chicago was "a grim, decaying city" that "was failing on nearly every measure." Renn elaborates: "The city was losing people, losing businesses, and losing jobs.... Manufacturing was collapsing and the middle class was fleeing, leading to neighborhood decline and eroding the city's tax base, which in turn degraded the city services residents had come to expect and demand. The decline in services and neighborhoods drove more people away, which led to further declines, perpetuating a vicious cycle."[184]

In a similar vein, *Chicago Tribune* correspondent Richard Longworth, author of a powerful front-page series in 1981 titled "A City on the Brink," concluded: "Chicago has become an economic invalid. The situation may be permanent." University of Illinois at Chicago Professor Pierre de Vise, for his part, saw "very little hope for locating economic activities here again." And a local

---

[183] http://www.city-journal.org/2012/22_2_chicago.html

[184] http://www.urbanophile.com/2012/06/24/state-of-chicago-the-decline-and-rise/

business executive asked, "Is the city being annihilated? It's probably inevitable."[185] The economic malaise that plagued Chicago during this period was accompanied by a steep decline in the city's population, which fell from 3.62 million in 1950 to 2.78 million by 1990.[186]

Harold Washington, an African American who served as Chicago's mayor from 1983-87, was an icon of the progressive left that now dominates the city's politics. Washington's election represented a break from the postwar Democratic Party machine whose symbolic figure was the first Mayor Richard Daley (Daley's son by the same name also became mayor of Chicago). Daley was one of the last of the big-city "bosses" who angered the left—especially with his zero-tolerance policy toward demonstrators at the 1968 Democratic Party convention—but his critics admitted that he presided over "a city that worked." Harold Washington was in effect the anti-Daley—an influence on the rising young local activist Barack Obama and on Obama's pastor and mentor, Jeremiah Wright, who mobilized black and Hispanic voters in support of Washington's electoral campaigns.

Close to the Chicago contingent of the Democratic Socialists of America, Washington calculated that he could most effectively advance his leftist agendas by calling himself a "liberal" and working within the Democratic Party. Unlike the first Mayor Daley, who used his immense power to make the machinery of city government run smoothly,

---

[185] http://www.urbanophile.com/2012/06/24/state-of-chicago-the-decline-and-rise/
[186] http://physics.bu.edu/~redner/projects/population/cities/chicago.html

Washington prioritized ideology. Stanley Kurtz, author and senior fellow at the Ethics and Public Policy Center who has closely followed Chicago politics, explains that Washington rose to political prominence by assembling "a 'rainbow' coalition of blacks, Hispanics, and left-leaning whites" whose ultimate aim was to "pus[h] the Democrats to the left by polarizing the country along class lines."[187]

During his 1983 campaign, Washington vowed to reduce regressive local taxes and rely more heavily on money from the State of Illinois. Once elected, however, he raised taxes on Chicagoans by hundreds of millions of dollars.[188] As one of his constituents later said, "All he did was tax, tax, tax."[189] Through a 1985 executive order, Washington enacted one of his major priorities as mayor: the implementation of an aggressive affirmative action program setting aside at least 25% of all city contracts for minority-owned business enterprises and another 5% for women-owned businesses.[190]

Under Washington, whose mayoralty ended suddenly in November 1987 when he died of a heart attack just a few months into his second term, Chicago's civic life

---

[187] http://www.frontpagemag.com/2011/stanley-kurtz/radical-in-chief-3/; http://www.nationalreview.com/articles/249390/obama%C3%ADs-radical-past-stanley-kurtz

[188] http://articles.chicagotribune.com/1987-02-08/news/8701100450_1_jane-byrne-tax-increases-city-taxes

[189] http://articles.chicagotribune.com/1987-11-30/news/8703300109_1_prayed-late-mayor-harold-washington

[190] https://www.isba.org/committees/minorities/newsletter/2009/11/thecityofchicagorenewsitscommitmenttominorityandw; http://articles.chicagotribune.com/1987-05-30/news/8702090883_1_city-contracts-civil-rights-law-mayor-harold-washington

deteriorated rapidly. One clear example involved the Chicago Housing Authority—a massive municipal agency that had been created to own and operate public housing built by the federal government—which was brought to the brink of insolvency by Washington's appointees.[191] The U.S. Secretary of Education in 1987 described the city's school system—where students were mostly poor and nonwhite—as the very worst in America.[192] Also during Mayor Washington's tenure, crime rates in the city exploded: Between 1982 and 1987, the annual incidence of robbery rose by 44%, while the corresponding increases for other crimes included 37% for burglary, more than 20% for both larceny-theft and auto theft, over 40% for arson, and at least 300% for aggravated assault.[193] Because this violent environment was toxic to local retail and service establishments, many business owners simply pulled up their roots and relocated to more welcoming places. All told, Chicago suffered a net loss of 45,000+ jobs during the '80s—a period of great economic prosperity and employment growth for most of the country—and many of the Windy City's job losses occurred on Mayor Washington's watch.[194] Likewise, Chicago's overall population declined,

---

[191] http://www.nytimes.com/1987/11/26/opinion/harold-washington-s-chicago.html

[192] http://articles.chicagotribune.com/2013-12-13/opinion/ct-emanuel-byrd-bennett-cps-education-perception-s-20131213_1_cps-schools-chicago-public-schools-mayor-and-schools-chief; http://www.nytimes.com/1987/11/26/opinion/harold-washington-s-chicago.html

[193] https://archive.org/stream/uniformcrimerepo1982unit#page/n7/mode/2up; https://archive.org/stream/uniformcrimerepoa1987unit#page/74/mode/2up

[194] http://articles.chicagotribune.com/1990-08-19/news/9003090558_1_service-sector-manufacturing-jobs-state-employment-data

on average, by more than 20,000 residents per year.[195]

Under Mayor Richard M. Daley (1989-2011), son and namesake of Mayor Richard J. Daley, Chicago rebounded a bit in the 1990s when it enjoyed a lower unemployment rate and stronger per-capita income growth than either New York or Los Angeles. It also added some 560,000 new jobs and gained more than 100,000 residents. During that same period, Chicago spent billions of dollars on a host of development projects including the construction of an elevated train line to Midway Airport, a wide-ranging street-beautification initiative, and the creation of impressive cultural facilities such as the $450 million Millennium Park.[196]

But in the first decade of the 21st century, these successes faded. Fiscal mismanagement by the Daley administration began to manifest itself in Chicago's economy, causing 7.1% of the city's jobs to dry up and disappear. Chicago's famous Loop, the second-largest central business district in the nation, was especially hard hit—losing 18.6% of its private-sector jobs. The city government, meanwhile, began incurring massive levels of debt, running an annual budget deficit of approximately $650 million.[197]

Contributing heavily to these shortfalls were ever-escalating expenditures on lavish benefits and pensions for

---

[195] http://physics.bu.edu/~redner/projects/population/cities/chicago.html

[196] http://www.city-journal.org/2012/22_2_chicago.html

[197] http://www.city-journal.org/2012/22_2_chicago.html; http://www.cdobs.com/archive/crime/demography-and-the-shellacking-of-chicago/

Chicago's public-sector union employees, whose political support had been decisive in the succession of Democrat mayoral administrations. The employee pensions were, by mandate of the Illinois state constitution, permanently immune to cutbacks.[198] According to the *Washington Post*, Chicago today owes nearly $14 billion in outstanding General Obligation bond debt,[199] and the city's pension funds owe $27 billion in unfunded obligations to police, firefighters, teachers, and municipal employees who have been courted—and rewarded—by administrations since the time of the first Mayor Daley. This shortfall amounts to more than $9,900 per city resident.[200] In Chicago's fire department alone, unfunded liabilities exceed 650% of payroll, meaning that they total more than 6.5 times what the city spends each year to pay all of its active firefighters. Similarly, the Chicago police department's unfunded liabilities amount to just above 600% of payroll.[201]

In 2008, Mayor Richard M. Daley sought to address his city's budget deficit, in part, by means of his now-infamous parking-meter lease, whereby—in exchange for $1.1 billion up front—the city sold its right to 75 years worth of parking revenues to the private company Chicago Parking Meters LLC. Just two years into the deal, the city had already spent 84% of that $1.1 billion and was looking

---

[198] http://www.city-journal.org/2012/22_2_chicago.html

[199] http://www.washingtonpost.com/blogs/govbeat/wp/2013/11/18/chicagos-mind-blowing-33-billion-debt-and-pension-obligations/

[200] http://www.huffingtonpost.com/2013/12/10/chicagos-own-pension-cris_n_4418720.html

[201] http://www.chicagobusiness.com/article/20130521/BLOGS02/130529975/city-halls-pension-spiral-worsens#

at the loss of countless billions in revenue over the next seven decades.[202]

Also in typical Democrat fashion, Chicago politicos have repeatedly sought to balance their budgets by raising local property and sales taxes. Today, Chicago has the nation's highest sales tax rate, whose impact on the city is amplified by Illinois' already-high state taxes.[203] According to a March 2013 *Wall Street Journal* report, the state and local taxes currently paid by Chicagoans are higher than those paid by their counterparts in all but four other American cities.[204] This oppressive tax climate has dealt a painful blow to Chicago's residents and business owners alike.

In July 2013, Moody's Investors Service—citing Chicago's "very large and growing pension liabilities and accelerating budget pressures associated with those liabilities"—downgraded the city's General Obligation (GO) and sales-tax ratings from AA3 to A3.[205] Four months later, another major ratings agency—Fitch Ratings, Inc.—likewise downgraded Chicago's debt worthiness after the

---

[202] http://www.huffingtonpost.com/2013/07/17/chicago-parking-meter-dea_n_3612219.html; http://www.city-journal.org/2012/22_2_chicago.html; http://theexpiredmeter.com/tag/chicago-parking-meter-lease-deal/

[203] http://www.city-journal.org/2012/22_2_chicago.html

[204] http://www.nbcchicago.com/news/local/Chicagoans-Pay-Fifth-Highest-Taxes-194516951.html

[205] http://www.washingtonpost.com/blogs/govbeat/wp/2013/11/18/chicagos-mind-blowing-33-billion-debt-and-pension-obligations/; https://www.moodys.com/research/Moodys-downgrades-Chicago-to-A3-from-Aa3-affecting-82-billion--PR_278069

Illinois legislature failed to pass a budget fix.²⁰⁶

Another factor harming small businesses in Chicago is the system of "aldermanic privilege" that dominates the city's politics and serves as a fertile breeding ground for corruption. As urban-affairs analyst Aaron Renn explains, Chicago's aldermen—i.e., city council members—have "nearly dictatorial control over what happens in their wards, from zoning changes to sidewalk café permits." As Renn notes, "This dumps political risk onto the shoulders of every would-be entrepreneur, who knows that he must stay on the alderman's good side to be in business. It's also a recipe for sleaze: 31 aldermen have been convicted of corruption since 1970."²⁰⁷ According to a University of Illinois report issued in 2012, Chicago is the most politically corrupt city in the United States, having averaged 51 public corruption convictions annually since 1976.²⁰⁸

Chicago's entrepreneurs are further handicapped by the byzantine regulations and red tape that make it prohibitively expensive and complicated to run a business within the city's confines. According to Chicagoland Chamber of Commerce CEO Jerry Roper, such "unnecessary and burdensome regulation" has placed Chicago "at a competitive disadvantage with other cities."²⁰⁹ The U.S.

---

²⁰⁶ http://articles.chicagotribune.com/2013-11-11/news/ct-met-chicago-bond-rating-1112-20131112_1_government-worker-pension-pension-issue-pension-problem

²⁰⁷ http://www.city-journal.org/2012/22_2_chicago.html

²⁰⁸ http://www.csmonitor.com/USA/Politics/2012/0215/Chicago-area-called-most-corrupt-in-US.-Why-Rahm-Emanuel-is-under-fire;

²⁰⁹ http://www.city-journal.org/2012/22_2_chicago.html

Chamber of Commerce, for its part, has described the litigation environment of Cook County—where Chicago is located—as the most unfair and unreasonable of any jurisdiction in the United States.[210]

Yet another reality that has had a severely negative impact on life in Chicago is violent crime. Since the mid-1970s, the annual homicide tally within the Windy City has ranged between 435 and 970, with the trends and fluctuations more-or-less mirroring those observable nationwide.[211] In 2012 and 2013, Chicago led all U.S. cities in homicides, with a combined total of 931 during that two-year period—far more than any other American city. In 2012, approximately one in every 1,000 Chicagoans was shot (either fatally or non-fatally) at some point during that year—a rate 6 times higher than in New York City.[212]

Whites, who constitute roughly 28% of Chicago's population, commit about 4% of all homicides in the city. African Americans, who are 35% of the population, are responsible for three-fourths of the homicides. The statistics for Chicago's black youth, many of whom have become involved in a culture of gang violence, are paricularly grim. Between 2003 and 2008, black youngsters accounted for 78% of all juvenile arrests in the city.[213]

---

[210] http://articles.chicagotribune.com/2012-09-10/business/chi-legal-climate-clouds-business-in-illinois-4-other-states-20120910_1_survey-legal-climate-institute-for-legal-reform

[211] http://en.wikipedia.org/wiki/Crime_in_Chicago#Homicides_in_Chicago_by_year

[212] http://pjmedia.com/blog/march-mayhem-mayor-never-waste-a-crisis-oversees-chicago-free-fall/

[213] http://www.city-journal.org/2010/20_1_chicago-crime.html

Driving the trend of stratospheric crime rates in Chicago's black community is a high incidence of single motherhood. Between 75% and 80% of the city's black children are born out-of-wedlock.[214] For decades, empirical research has demonstrated conclusively that growing up without a father is a far better forecaster of a boy's future criminality than either race or poverty. Indeed, regardless of race, 70% of all young people in state reform institutions were raised in fatherless homes, as were 60% of rapists, 72% of adolescent murderers, and 70% of long-term prison inmates.[215]

In recent years, Chicago has been the scene of dozens of violent, black-on-white "flash mob" attacks, as documented by author Colin Flaherty. One of the most recent, high-profile incidents occurred at the end of March 2013, when some 500 blacks stormed the so-called Magnificent Mile, an upscale shopping area, randomly assaulting innocent people and destroying property.[216]

The response of Chicago's leadership to this type of criminality has been far less assertive than that of New York, for instance, where Republican Mayor Rudolph Giuliani and Police Chief William Bratton in the 1990s instituted a proactive, aggressive, and highly successful anti-crime strategy that incorporated "stop-and-frisk"

---

[214] http://www.city-journal.org/2010/20_1_chicago-crime.html

[215] http://articles.latimes.com/1992-05-07/local/me-2237_1_young-black-men; Mona Charen, "Liberal Tinkering Has Put Our Civilization at Risk," *Conservative Chronicle* (August 24, 1994), p. 21.

[216] http://www.frontpagemag.com/2013/colin-flaherty/chicago-running-out-of-euphemisms/

policies and so-called "broken windows" law-enforcement philosophy. Their approach—which was subsequently continued, to similar effect, by Giuliani's Republican successor Michael Bloomberg—reversed a long trend of escalating criminality that had plagued New York City in the pre-Giuliani years.[217]

By contrast, Chicago's politicians, community activists, and religious leaders alike have largely turned their backs on such policing philosophies. As a former Chicago deputy superintendent of police once observed: "Mayor Daley [who served from 1989-2011] is not a cop supporter."[218]

Chicago's failure to establish control over either its economy or its crime problem is mirrored by the persistent inability of its lavishly funded public-school system to educate the city's children. There is little to show for the more than $13,000 spent annually on the education-related expenses of each K-12 student in the city.[219] In the 2013 National Assessment of Educational Progress (NAEP), standardized exams designed to measure students' academic abilities:

- Just 21% of Chicago fourth-graders performed well enough to be classified as "proficient" or better in grade-level reading—vs. 34% of fourth-graders

---

[217] http://www.discoverthenetworks.org/viewSubCategory.asp?id=1633; http://www.discoverthenetworks.org/viewSubCategory.asp?id=1629

[218] http://www.city-journal.org/2010/20_1_chicago-crime.html

[219] http://www.chicagonow.com/windy-city-young-republicans/2012/04/chicago-public-schools-by-the-numbers/

nationally.[220]

- Only 27% of Chicago fourth-graders performed well enough to be classified as "proficient" or better in grade-level math—vs. 42% of fourth-graders nationally.[221]
- A mere 20% of Chicago eighth-graders performed well enough to be categorized as "proficient" or better in grade-level reading, vs. 35% of eighth-graders nationally.[222]
- Just 20% of Chicago eighth-graders performed well enough to be deemed "proficient" or better in grade-level math, vs. 34% of eighth-graders nationally.[223]

Moreover, only 63% of Chicago's public high-school students graduate on time (within four years)—well below the national average of 78%.[224]

In June 2013, Chicago Teachers Union president Karen Lewis, a Democrat, attributed the failures of the Chicago Public Schools not to any shortcomings in the city's educational apparatus, but rather to the "fact that rich white people think they know what's in the best interest of

---

[220] http://nces.ed.gov/nationsreportcard/subject/publications/dst2013/pdf/2014467XC4.pdf

[221] http://nces.ed.gov/nationsreportcard/subject/publications/dst2013/pdf/2014468xc4.pdf

[222] http://nces.ed.gov/nationsreportcard/subject/publications/dst2013/pdf/2014467XC8.pdf

[223] http://nces.ed.gov/nationsreportcard/subject/publications/dst2013/pdf/2014468xc8.pdf

[224] http://www.nbcchicago.com/blogs/ward-room/chicago-high-school-graduation-rate-63-percent-209156451.html

children of African-Americans and Latinos, no matter what the parents' income or education level." She elaborated on this charge that racism caused educational failure: "If you look at the majority of the tax base for property taxes in Chicago, they're mostly white, who don't have a real interest in paying for the education of poor black and brown children."[225]

Following a pattern that is seen repeatedly in Democrat-controlled cities across the United States, Chicago's toxic brew of high taxes, out-of-control crime rates, failing schools, mounting public debt, and anti-business economic climate has driven away massive numbers of residents and entrepreneurs. After the city's population peaked at 3.62 million in 1950,[226] it underwent a half-century of decline that leveled off only temporarily in the 1990s. In the first decade of the 21st century, some 200,000 people (including 175,000 African Americans) moved out of Chicago—an exodus exceeded in magnitude only in Detroit.[227] According to the 2010 U.S. Census Bureau Report, Chicago's population was 2,695,598 and falling.[228]

---

[225] http://www.breitbart.com/Big-Government/2013/06/19/Chicago-Teachers-Union-rich-white

[226] http://online.wsj.com/news/articles/SB10001424052748703312904576146741729857936

[227] http://articles.chicagotribune.com/2011-02-15/news/ct-met-2010-census-20110215_1_census-data-collar-counties-population; http://www.city-journal.org/2012/22_2_chicago.html

[228] http://online.wsj.com/ncws/articles/SB10001424052748703312904576146741729857936

Milwaukee

For years it was the world's foremost beer-producing city, home to four of the largest breweries in the world (Schlitz, Blatz, Pabst, and Miller). Almost every major American brewery, in fact, had at least one factory in Milwaukee. These employed thousands of local residents in jobs that formed the foundation of the city's solid middle class.[229] Other major corporations in the city during the first half of the twentieth century included the A. F. Gallun & Sons leather tanning company; the machinery manufacturer Allis-Chalmers; the heavy-mining equipment producer Bucyrus Erie Company; the Falk Corporation, producer of industrial power transmission products; the electrical component maker Cutler-Hammer; and the A.O. Smith Corporation, a major manufacturer of automotive frames.[230]

Most of them are gone now and Milwaukee is a different place.

Every Milwaukee mayor of the past 106 years has been a Democrat—with the exception of three who were Socialists. The first of the Socialists—in fact the first Socialist mayor of any major American city—was Emil Seidel, who held office from 1910-12. Next came Daniel Webster Hoan in 1916, whose 24-year tenure in office

---

[229] http://www.jsonline.com/news/opinion/a-look-at-the-decline-of-milwaukees-middle-class-b9949923z1-214822101.html

[230] http://www.pbs.org/wgbh/pages/frontline/business-economy-financial-crisis/two-american-families/photos-milwaukees-industrial-past/

was the longest continuous Socialist administration in American history. The city's third Socialist mayor was Frank Paul Zeidler, who served three terms from 1948-60 and whose administration oversaw the large-scale construction of public housing as a means of promoting racial and economic justice.[231]

Zeidler spoke out forcefully in favor of what he termed "public enterprise," the notion that government could improve the condition of the poor via the efficient dispensation of taxpayer-funded public services.[232] But demographic trends capsized this theory. During Zeidler's time in office, Milwaukee's black population nearly quintupled, from 13,000 in 1945 to more than 62,000 in 1960, as Southern blacks began their northward migration away from segregation and toward jobs. They were packed into a few areas as a result of "de facto" segregation.[233]

Local black radicals, allied ideologically with the black militancy that was sweeping many American cities in the Sixties, were dissatisfied with what they viewed as the inadequate pace of racial reforms. And in the summer of 1967, the race riots that rocked Detroit and Newark sparked a similar—though less devastating—outburst in Milwaukee which resulted in 3 deaths, about 100 injuries, and 1,740 arrests.[234]

---

[231] http://tinyurl.com/nnja5ke

[232] http://www.democraticunderground.com/discuss/duboard.php?az=view_all&address=103x223344

[233] http://www.milwaukechistory.net/education/milwaukee-timeline/

[234] http://www.milwaukeehistory.net/education/milwaukee-timeline/

In response to the rioting, Democrat Henry Maier, who served as mayor of Milwaukee from 1960-88, swiftly unveiled a "39-Point Program" designed to address the inner-city problems of poverty and racism that liberal Democrats widely cited as the causes of the riots. This program was based on pouring massive amounts of local, state, and federal money into initiatives like housing construction, youth programs, and "community renewal" to pacify an angry populace.[235] But in the eyes of local black leftists, it was too little, too late. As Mrs. Vel Phillips, a black member of Milwaukee's Common Council, said in April 1968, the mayor's 39-point program had failed to demonstrate any "visible effect on the root causes" of ghetto unrest: "I don't believe in violence, and I hope we don't have any more. But we'd all better realize that many young Negroes have reached the point where they're ready and willing to die because they figure they have nothing to lose."[236]

As of 1970, seven of Milwaukee's top ten companies were engaged in manufacturing and employed nearly 47,000 people.[237] But as the cost of manufacturing in the U.S. skyrocketed in subsequent decades and the city became fiscally inhospitable many of these businesses moved their operations. Between 1970 and 2011, Milwaukee lost no fewer than 40% of its manufacturing jobs—a severe

---

[235] http://www.milwaukeehistory.net/education/milwaukee-timeline/; http://news.google.com/newspapers?nid=1368&dat=19680109&id=QX9QAAAAIBAJ&sjid=mRAEAAAAIBAJ&pg=6074,2636309

[236] http://www.newspapers.com/newspage/45005251/

[237] http://www.jsonline.com/news/opinion/a-look-at-the-decline-of-milwaukees-middle-class-b9949923z1-214822101.html

economic blow to the entire city. From 1970 to 2007, the percentage of families in the Milwaukee metro area that were middle-class declined from 37% to 24%, while the percentage of households that were poor spiked from 23% to 31%.[238]

Today, per capita income in Milwaukee is $19,199 (32% below the national average); median household income is $35,823 (33% below the national average); and the poverty rate is 28.3% (nearly double the national average).[239]

While joblessness and poverty plague many Milwaukeeans, crime may be an even larger affliction in their lives. Milwaukee today has a violent crime rate that is 2.6 times greater than the national average, including a robbery rate of 4.4 times the national average and a murder rate that is triple the national average.[240] In 2012, 80% of all homicide victims in the city were black, as were three-fourths of the known suspects in these crimes.[241]

Though the city's public school system annually spends some $14,200 (about one-third more than the national average) in taxpayer funds on the education of each

---

[238] http://www.theatlantic.com/business/archive/2011/12/free-falling-in-milwaukee-a-close-up-on-one-citys-middle-class-decline/250100/

[239] http://quickfacts.census.gov/qfd/states/55/5553000.html; http://quickfacts.census.gov/qfd/states/00000.html

[240] http://www.city-data.com/crime/crime-Milwaukee-Wisconsin.html

[241] http://www.wnd.com/2013/08/milwaukees-racism-most-murders-black-on-black/

K-12 student in its jurisdiction,[242] the overall high-school graduation rate in the Milwaukee Public Schools (MPS) is a paltry 62.8%—far below Wisconsin's 87% statewide average.[243] On standardized National Assessment of Educational Progress (NAEP) tests administered in 2013 to measure students' academic abilities:

- Only 18% of Milwaukee's fourth-graders scored as proficient or better in math.[244]
- Just 11% of Milwaukee's eighth-graders scored as proficient or better in math.[245]
- A mere 16% of Milwaukee's fourth-graders scored as proficient or better in reading.[246]
- Only 13% of Milwaukee's eighth-graders scored as proficient or better in reading.[247]

But unlike their counterparts in other cities, some Milwaukee students, thanks to a handful of civic leaders and activists as well as vital funding from the Bradley Foundation, have access to a school voucher program. In

---

[242] http://www.jsonline.com/news/education/mps-wisconsin-rank-high-in-per-pupil-spending-b9915750z1-208377331.html; http://www.jsonline.com/news/education/mps-wisconsin-rank-high-in-per-pupil-spending-b9915750z1-208377331.html

[243] http://www.jsonline.com/news/education/state-mps-post-improved-high-school-graduation-rates-875f3om-151883025.html

[244] http://nces.ed.gov/nationsreportcard/subject/publications/dst2013/pdf/2014468XK4.pdf

[245] http://nces.ed.gov/nationsreportcard/subject/publications/dst2013/pdf/2014468XK8.pdf

[246] http://nces.ed.gov/nationsreportcard/subject/publications/dst2013/pdf/2014467XK4.pdf

[247] http://nces.ed.gov/nationsreportcard/subject/publications/dst2013/pdf/2014467XK8.pdf

response to a long effort by this group of advocates, in 1990 the Wisconsin State Legislature passed a bill creating the Milwaukee Parental Choice Program (MPCP), the first publicly funded voucher initiative in the United States.[248] Though lawmakers initially restricted it to just 1,000 low-income public school students within the city, MPCP has since grown, largely as a result of private fundraising, to become the largest voucher program in America, serving more than 20,000 students.[249] A 2011 study published by School Choice Wisconsin indicated that students in the MPCP had a graduation rate 18% higher than their counterparts in the Milwaukee Public Schools.[250] Showing also that the massive per-pupil outlays championed by teachers' unions are unnecessary to increase achievement, the MPCP spends $6,442 per scholarship to educate its students—less than half of what the non-voucher public schools spend.[251]

The Democrat-controlled teachers' unions have fought the MPCP tooth-and-nail.[252] So has a group called the Educators' Network for Social Justice (ENSJ), a leftist alliance of classroom teachers and post-secondary instructors who have allied themselves with the Democratic Party of Milwaukee County and a number of local Democrat

---

[248] http://www.city-journal.org/html/9_1_a1.html

[249] http://blog.heritage.org/2011/01/12/voucher-students-soar-in-milwaukee/

[250] http://www.businesswire.com/news/home/20100202006097/en/Study-Graduation-Rate-Milwaukee-Voucher-Students-18#.U2ARR2ByFWM

[251] http://www.businesswire.com/news/home/20100202006097/en/Study-Graduation-Rate-Milwaukee-Voucher-Students-18#.U2ARR2ByFWM; http://blog.heritage.org/2011/01/12/voucher-students-soar-in-milwaukee/

[252] http://www.city-journal.org/html/9_1_a1.html

politicians. Committed to "promoting pro-justice curricula and policies so that all students in the Milwaukee area are better served," ENSJ also opposes the use of standardized tests to measure student achievement and aptitude.[253]

The poverty, crime, unemployment, and dysfunctional school system that have become the hallmarks of life in Milwaukee have led the city's population to decline markedly in recent decades, from 741,000 in 1960 to just 599,000 today.[254] An estimated 5,000 houses—mostly in impoverished neighborhoods—stand vacant and abandoned, a mute testament to peoples' desire to get out of town.[255]

Newark

The city of Newark, New Jersey has been led exclusively by Democrat mayors for the past 81 years. The entrenched power of the Democratic Party is reflected in the near-unanimous support its candidates receive from Newark voters in political elections on every level. For example, in the 2009 gubernatorial race, Newark voters cast 90.2% of their ballots for Democrat Jon Corzine, vs. just 8.3%

---

[253] http://www.discoverthenetworks.org/groupProfile.asp?grpid=7777;

[254] http://www.infoplease.com/ipa/A0922422.html; http://quickfacts.census.gov/qfd/states/55/5553000.html

[255] http://www.milwaukeemag.com/article/1222014-AbandonedDreams

for Republican Chris Christie, the ultimate winner.[256] And in the 2008 presidential election, Democrat Barack Obama captured 90.8% of the Newark vote, vs. 7.0% for Republican John McCain.[257]

At one time, Newark was bustling and prosperous. As of 1922, it had 63 live theaters and 46 movie theaters, and its so-called "Four Corners"—where Market and Broad Streets intersected—was widely considered the busiest intersection in the country. In 1927, a prominent businessman observed: "Great is Newark's vitality. It is the red blood in its veins—this basic strength that is going to carry it over whatever hurdles it may encounter, enable it to recover from whatever losses it may suffer and battle its way to still higher achievement industrially and financially, making it eventually perhaps the greatest industrial center in the world."[258] The realities of Newark today make these words sound like they were written in a foreign language.

Between 1950 and 1967, Newark's black population rose from 70,000 to 220,000, largely as a result of the arrival of African Americans leaving the segregated south for northern job opportunities. Newark educator Nathan Wright Jr. noted that "no typical American city has as yet experienced such a precipitous change from a white to a

---

[256] http://www.state.nj.us/state/elections/election-results/2009-governor_results-essex.pdf

[257] http://www.state.nj.us/state/elections/election-results/2008-gen-elect-presidential-results-essex.pdf

[258] http://books.google.com/books?id=lwave_qPlYUC&pg=PA275&lpg=PA275&dq=#v=onepage&q&f=false

black majority."[259]

In response to the influx, the city's Democratic leadership launched major urban-renewal initiatives during the 1960s, persuading the federal government to cover 100% of the costs associated with constructing new public housing projects. Eventually, Newark had a higher percentage of its residents living in public housing than any other city in the United States.[260]

Black militants in the city, however, derided this and other costly programs that displaced some black residential neighborhoods as "Negro removal." The militants were angered by plans to build superhighways that would bisect the city's black community. They likewise condemned a proposal in early 1967 for the "clearance" of 150 acres of predominantly black "slum" land on which a medical school/hospital complex would be built.[261] In 1967, the rage of Newark's black militants exploded in the form of devastating race riots. The incident precipitating the violence was the police beating of a black cabbie on the night of July 12, 1967. The rioting persisted for six days and resulted in 23 deaths, 725 injuries, nearly 1,500 arrests, $10 million in property damage, and the destruction of approximately 1,000 stores and business establishments.[262] As was the case in other cities that experienced similar

---

[259] http://tinyurl.com/npm34lg

[260] http://en.wikipedia.org/wiki/History_of_Newark,_New_Jersey

[261] http://tinyurl.com/ltb4pcc

[262] http://scholar.library.miami.edu/sixtiesChron/ch07.html; http://webatomics.com/jason/Images/thesisone.pdf

violence during this era, Newark never really recovered from these riots.

In addition to the race problem, Newark was also struggling with political corruption. The city's politics have been plagued by Mob influence for generations. According to the *City Journal*, for instance, the bootlegger Abner "Longy" Zwillman, who smuggled through Newark nearly 40% of all the liquor sold on the East Coast during Prohibition, "bought off enough local officials to take control of the city's politics from the late 1920s until his death in 1959."[263] In 1962, Angelo "Ray" DeCarlo, a capo in New York's Genovese crime family, helped fix the Newark mayoral election for Democrat Hugh Addonizio. "Federal investigations into Addonizio's sleazy administration later revealed that almost every aspect of Newark's government operated like a racket," writes Manhattan Institute scholar Steven Malanga. "Officials fattened the cost of contracts by 10 percent for kickbacks, and city government even used the same bought-and-paid-for auditors as the mob did. Every Newark citizen and firm paid a corruption tax." Partly because of this, Newark at that time had the most expensive government of any midsize American city—spending almost twice as much per capita as the average urban area.[264] By 1967, Newark's property tax rate was $7.75 per $100 of assessed value, the highest in America. As the Newark *Star-Ledger* notes: "If taxed at that rate today, an average home in New Jersey—valued at $350,000—would owe more than $27,000 a year in

---

[263] http://www.city-journal.org/html/17_2_cory_booker.html
[264] http://www.city-journal.org/html/17_2_cory_booker.html

property taxes."[265]

Lawlessness in high places, in conjunction with escalating costs and a volatile racial atmosphere, made Newark an increasingly undesirable place to live. "Fearful and without faith in Newark's blatantly crooked government," writes Steven Malanga, "the middle class fled. The city's population shrank to just 270,000 mostly low-income residents—a 40 percent decline."[266] Throughout the 1950s and '60s, manufacturers and entrepreneurs in Newark pulled up their roots and sought out other locations that were less expensive, more business-friendly, and less socially combustible. Between 1950 and 1960, the city's white population fell by nearly a third, from 363,000 to 265,000.[267]

Addonizio's successor was Kenneth Gibson, the city's first black mayor. Amiri Baraka—the black nationalist, anti-Semitic poet/playwright, and self-avowed Marxist-Leninist—played a key role in galvanizing black voters to support Gibson at the polls. "We will nationalize the city's institutions, as if it were liberated territory in Zimbabwe or Angola," Baraka declared at the time.[268]

Upon his election, Gibson boldly proclaimed: "Wherever American cities are going, Newark will get

---

[265] http://blog.nj.com/ledgernewark/2007/07/crossroads_part_1.html
[266] http://www.city-journal.org/html/17_2_cory_booker.html
[267] http://www.city-journal.org/html/17_2_cory_booker.html; http://webatomics.com/jason/Images/thesisone.pdf
[268] http://tinyurl.com/k9vcwxa

there first."[269] Gibson was right: Newark would lead the rush toward insolvency, corruption and racial conflict that marked America's future urban reality. Contradicting the expectations of Baraka and other radical intellectuals who had supported him, the new mayor inaugurated policies that had a strong negative impact on blacks and the poor in Newark. The city continued to hemorrhage industrial jobs, as employment rates declined and the welfare rolls swelled. As more and more factories were abandoned, the number of taxable properties in the city decreased, cutting sharply into the city's income and bringing it to the threshold of bankruptcy several times. Neighborhood programs and services—including trash collection—were cut repeatedly throughout the '70s. Indeed, massive, stinking piles of uncollected garbage became a dismaying symbol of life in Newark during the decade.[270]

Gibson's administration was also afflicted by significant corruption. In 1982, investigators jailed numerous city officials for various infractions. Gibson himself faced state charges of having conspired to create a no-show job specifically for a former Newark official but was acquitted in 1982.[271] By 1986, Gibson's last year in office, the city's unemployment rate was nearly 50% higher than it had been at the start of his mayoralty. A Manhattan Institute report states that by the end of Gibson's tenure in office, "failed government policies and middle-class flight had weakened

---

[269] http://news.google.com/newspapers?nid=799&dat=19730308&id=jVgzAAAAIBAJ&sjid=WlIDAAAAIBAJ&pg=700,4399913

[270] http://webatomics.com/jason/Images/thesisone.pdf

[271] http://www.nytimes.com/2005/01/30/nyregion/30folo.html?_r=0

much of Newark, except for a few corporate-supported blocks downtown and a few enclaves...."[272]

Every Newark mayor since Gibson has also been African American. His successor in 1986 was Democrat Sharpe James, who went on to hold office for two decades. Conditions in James's own neighborhood, the South Ward, were particularly grim—replete with decrepit, crime-infested public housing projects and hundreds of vacant lots.[273]

The James administration became infamous for its corruption. In 1996, for instance, Newark's police commissioner pled guilty to stealing money that had been intended to finance local undercover narcotics investigations.[274] The following year, the mayor's chief of staff, Jackie Mattison, was convicted of taking bribes to help steer city contracts to a particular insurance broker.[275] And during his final term in office, James himself sold a number of the city's publicly owned vacant lots to his friends and supporters—for pennies on the dollar. One of the buyers was James's mistress, Tamika Riley, who between 2001 and 2005 spent a grand total of $46,000 to purchase nine tracts of land from the city, which in each instance she promptly resold for a large profit. All told, Ms. Riley collected

---

[272] http://www.manhattan-institute.org/email/crd_newsletter07-07.html
[273] http://www.manhattan-institute.org/email/crd_newsletter07-07.html
[274] http://www.city-journal.org/html/16_2_new_jersey.html
[275] http://www.nytimes.com/2007/07/14/nyregion/14james.html?fta=y&_r=0&gwh =C6CF51C78E8F7038AEC410DE2C97D0CB&gwt=pay

$665,000 from these sales.[276] For his involvement in this scam, James was convicted in 2008 on five counts of fraud and conspiracy charges; he subsequently spent 27 months in prison and was fined $100,000. Prosecutors dropped additional charges that James had billed the city for a host of personal expenses including meals, pornography, and body lotions, when they concluded that convictions for these items would not add any time to his prison sentence.[277]

Mayor James's ethical failure became standard operating procedure in Newark politics. Since 1962, every mayor of Newark except Cory Booker (2006- 2013) has been indicted for crimes committed while in office.[278]

Newark's woes are exacerbated by the fact that it is currently the second most highly taxed city in the United States. One study in 2013 estimated that the average three-person family with $50,000 in annual income owed $8,327 per year in local school and property taxes alone.[279]

Newark's unemployment rate is approximately two-thirds higher than that of New Jersey as a whole, and more

---

[276] http://www.nj.com/news/ledger/topstories/index.ssf/2008/04/newark_exmayor_sharpe_james_fo.html

[277] http://www.newsweek.com/swamps-jersey-69529; http://www.nj.com/news/ledger/topstories/index.ssf/2008/04/newark_exmayor_sharpe_james_fo.html; http://www.nj.com/news/index.ssf/2010/04/sharpe_james_is_released_from.html

[278] http://www.newsweek.com/swamps-jersey-69529

[279] http://blogs.hrblock.com/2013/02/05/the-top-10-most-taxed-cities-in-america-infographic/

than twice the national average.[280] Per capita income in Newark is just $17,161 per year (38% below the national average and less than half the New Jersey average), and median household income is $34,387 (about 36% below the national average).[281] The poverty rate citywide is 31%, and the child-advocacy organization New Jersey Kids Count estimates that about a quarter of Newark children under age 5 live in "extreme poverty."[282]

The city's disastrously ineffective public education system spends an astronomical $23,000 on each K-12 pupil in its jurisdiction.[283] But in tests that were administered to elementary through junior-high-school students in 2013, just 19% of Newark's third-graders registered scores indicating that they were "proficient" in English; the corresponding figure in math was 21%. The numbers were similar for students in grades 4 through 8.[284]

According to the New Jersey Department of Education, the dropout rate for Newark's high-school students is nearly 40%.[285] Among those who do manage to graduate, only

---

[280] http://www.huffingtonpost.com/2013/10/18/cory-booker-newark_n_4123455.html

[281] http://quickfacts.census.gov/qfd/states/34/3451000.html; http://quickfacts.census.gov/qfd/states/00000.html

[282] http://www.city-data.com/poverty/poverty-Newark-New-Jersey.html; http://www.huffingtonpost.com/2013/10/18/cory-booker-newark_n_4123455.html

[283] http://www.nj.com/news/index.ssf/2012/06/nj_school_report_cards_release.html

[284] http://www.waynepost.com/article/20130830/NEWS/130839998/10057/NEWS

[285] http://www.huffingtonpost.com/2013/10/18/cory-booker-newark_n_4123455.html

about 3-in-10 are able to pass a state proficiency exam indicating that they are qualified for college-level work. Dan Gaby, executive director of the education-reform group E3, puts these numbers in perspective by estimating that Newark taxpayers spend approximately *$1.3 million* on the education-related expenses of each *qualified* student who earns a diploma from one of the city's public high schools.[286]

Compounding the academic decline in Newark is the fact that the city's school district has been mismanaged into a state of financial chaos. At the start of the 2013-14 school year, the district faced a projected budget shortfall of $57 million.[287]

Perhaps the biggest drain on Newark's quality of life, however, is the city's high rate of violent crime—including a murder rate that is roughly 7.2 times the national average and a robbery rate of 6.2 times the national average.[288] Newark's criminal element has long understood that it can break the law with virtual impunity. As of 2007, the county prosecutor's office responsible for Newark had the worst conviction rate of any county in New Jersey—in part because, as the *City Journal* notes, it has been "a haven for political appointees who aren't necessarily qualified investigators or prosecutors."[289]

---

[286] http://www.city-journal.org/html/17_2_cory_booker.html

[287] http://www.edlawcenter.org/news/archives/school-funding/state-operated-newark-schools-face-staggering-$57-million-budget-deficit.html

[288] http://www.city-data.com/crime/crime-Newark-New-Jersey.html

[289] http://www.city-journal.org/html/17_2_cory_booker.html

In September 2011, the combination of high taxes and intolerable crime rates led a large group of angry residents, predominantly black, of Newark's East Ward, to stage a protest demonstration at city hall.[290] Many others, meanwhile, have protested with their feet. Newark's population, which stood at 429,760 in 1940, is just 77,000 today.[291]

St. Louis

During World War II, St. Louis, Missouri was a bustling place replete with factories that produced such necessities as ammunition, uniforms and footwear, K-rations, chemicals and medicines, and even aircraft. Soon after the war, in 1949, an era of Democratic rule began that continues in the city to this day. Indeed, it has been 65 years since a Republican was elected mayor of St. Louis. This entrenched Democratic dominance is reflected in the fact that in each of the past three U.S. presidential elections, voters in St. Louis cast between 80 and 84 percent of their ballots for the Democrat candidate.[292]

Between 1940 and 1970, St. Louis was one of the major destinations for the millions of blacks who migrated away from the rural South to take advantage of newly available

---

[290] http://www.nj.com/news/index.ssf/2011/09/high_taxes_rising_crime_push_n.html

[291] http://www.infoplease.com/ipa/A0922422.html

[292] http://www.city-data.com/city/St.-Louis-Missouri.html

job opportunities in Northern cities. During this 30-year period, St. Louis's black population nearly tripled, from approximately 108,000 to more than 317,000.[293] By 1970, it was a majority-black city—a fact that, in light of the overwhelming degree to which African Americans identify as Democrats, would have immense political implications for the city and its future.

The start of St. Louis's Democratic era, which began with the mayoralty of Joseph Darst, coincided with President Harry Truman's signing of the American Housing Act of 1949. This legislation greatly expanded the role of federal funds in the construction of public housing, and kick-started the "urban redevelopment" (also known as "urban renewal") programs that would reshape a host of American cities. Darst, like so many Democrats, was a strong proponent of such federal intervention in local affairs.[294] By the end of his four-year term as mayor, approximately 700 public housing units had been completed citywide, with an additional 17,000 under construction and 4,000 in the planning stages.

Darst's successor was Raymond Tucker, a longtime professor of mechanical engineering at Washington University, who went on to serve three terms as St. Louis mayor from 1953-65. The early part of his tenure coincided

---

[293] http://www.infoplease.com/ipa/A0922422.html; http://physics.bu.edu/~redner/projects/population/cities/stlouis.html; http://books.google.com/books?id=n7ixiFDFApAC&pg=PA11&lpg=PA11&dq=#v=onepage&q&f=false

[294] http://books.google.com/books?id=n7ixiFDFApAC&pg=PA51&lpg=PA51&dq=#v=onepage&q&f=false

with the passage of the Housing Act of 1954, which, under the authority of the Federal Housing Administration, was initially drafted to create 140,000 public housing units in cities across the U.S., including St. Louis. Like Darst before him, Tucker was a staunch believer in the transformative powers of urban renewal—a strategy that, in the words of University of Illinois political science professor Dennis Judd, "was now the big game in town."[295]

Amid this wave of optimism, St. Louis issued bonds in 1953 to finance the completion of the St. Louis Gateway Mall and a number of high-rise housing projects. The most famous of these was the federally funded Pruitt-Igoe housing project which consisted of 33 eleven-story buildings with nearly 3,000 units in total. But showering the local population with federal cash—a longstanding Democrat tradition—was not the recipe for lasting success its proponents hoped. Indeed, just a few years after Pruitt-Igoe first opened its doors in 1956, it fell into disrepair and became a hotbed of crime and vandalism. As Alexander von Hoffman of Harvard University's Joint Center for Housing Studies writes: "Large numbers of vacancies indicated that even poor people preferred to live anywhere but Pruitt-Igoe. In 1972, after spending more than $5 million in vain to cure the problems at Pruitt-Igoe, the St. Louis Housing Authority, in a highly publicized event, demolished three of the high-rise buildings. A year later, in concert with the U.S. Department of Housing and

---

[295] http://books.google.com/books?id=n7ixiFDFApAC&pg=PA51&lpg=PA51&dq=#v=onepage&q&f=false; http://books.google.com/books?id=XyXBLu-DolwC&pg=PA87&lpg=PA87&dq=#v=onepage&q&f=false

Urban Development, it declared Pruitt-Igoe unsalvageable and razed the remaining buildings."[296]

The Pruitt-Igoe experience was typical of urban renewal endeavors across the United States. By the time the urban renewal era ended in 1973, it was widely regarded as a colossal failure.[297]

During 1950-70, a period which coincided with the era of urban renewal, close to 60% of St. Louis's white residents relocated to other towns and cities.[298] According to University of Iowa history professor Colin Gordon, who authored the 2008 book *Mapping Decline: St. Louis and the Fate of the American City*, St. Louis during this period became "the poster child of white flight."[299]

But this was not simply a case of racial phobia. Gordon also notes that whites were not alone in their eagerness to escape St. Louis's crime-infested streets. "White flight in St. Louis was followed closely by black flight," he explains, "leaving large tracts of the North Side virtually vacant and much of the 'urban crisis' now located in North County's inner suburbs."[300] Between 1970 and 1980, as St. Louis's overall population fell from about 622,000 to just 453,000, the city's black population likewise declined from 317,000

---

[296] http://www.soc.iastate.edu/sapp/PruittIgoe.html
[297] http://www.encyclopedia.com/topic/Urban_renewal.aspx
[298] http://mappingdecline.lib.uiowa.edu/map/
[299] http://www.stlmag.com/St-Louis-Magazine/December-2008/Mapping-the-Divide/
[300] http://www.stlmag.com/St-Louis-Magazine/December-2008/Mapping-the-Divide/

to about 206,000.[301]

In 1993, St. Louis elected its first black mayor, Democrat Freeman Bosley Jr., whose four years in office were marked by a failure to deal with an exploding crime problem. From the beginning of his tenure in office, Bosley tried quixotically to arrange friendly meetings between himself and local gang members, urging them to stay in school and assuring them that he was "committed to finding you jobs." He convinced a number of corporate sponsors to offer 500 paying jobs to city students in the summer of 2004; he established eight community schools with recreation centers open until 10 p.m. each night, in an effort to help keep young people out of trouble; and city corporations bankrolled a Midnight Basketball League for similar purposes.[302] Notwithstanding all these efforts, Bosley's first year in office was the bloodiest in city history, with 267 homicides.[303]

By the end of the Nineties, social and economic decay were evident throughout much of St. Louis, as evidenced by the following excerpt from the 1999 St. Louis City Plan:

> "[A] visual survey of the neighborhood reveals a tree-lined block of stable, well-kept, two- and four-

---

[301] http://mappingdecline.lib.uiowa.edu/map/; http://books.google.com/books?id=X9XG-2fWgWcC&pg=PA207&lpg=PA207&dq=#v=onepage&q&f=false; https://www.census.gov/prod/www/decennial.html

[302] http://www.csmonitor.com/1994/0418/19021.html/(page)/2

[303] http://www.stlamerican.com/news/local_news/article_7a896a3a-29a1-11e0-b19d-001cc4c03286.html

family homes followed by a block of overgrown board-ups on a one-to-one ratio with intact housing.... Two blocks later, a once commercial area of St. Louis Avenue is now totally empty with vacated lots and derelict buildings. This trend is not specific to St. Louis Avenue; the same can be said of Taylor, Greer, Labadie, and most other neighborhood streets. For businesses, the situation appears even worse. Signs of life are few and far between the corner store board-ups and chain-link-fence-covered storefronts."[304]

By the year 2000, the total population of St. Louis—which had peaked at about 857,000 in 1950—had fallen to 348,000.[305] Remarkably, this figure was smaller than that which had been recorded in the city's census 120 years earlier.[306] According to New Geography.com: "Among the world's municipalities that have ever achieved 500,000 population, none have lost so much as the city of St. Louis."[307]

After decades of Democratic leadership, St. Louis today is a city facing severe economic challenges. It has a per capita income of just $22,551 (about 20% below the national average), a median household income of $34,384

---

[304] http://tinyurl.com/plf4gq7
[305] http://en.wikipedia.org/wiki/Largest_cities_in_the_United_States_by_population_by_decade#1950; http://mappingdecline.lib.uiowa.edu/map/
[306] http://en.wikipedia.org/wiki/Largest_cities_in_the_United_States_by_population_by_decade#1880
[307] http://www.newgeography.com/content/002078-city-st-louis-suffers-huge-population-loss

(some 35% below the national median), and a poverty rate of 27% (nearly twice the national average).[308]

According to *CQ Press,* which annually publishes crime rankings that compare cities across the United States in terms of their respective incidences of murder, rape, robbery, aggravated assault, burglary, and motor vehicle theft, St. Louis was "America's Most Dangerous City" in 2006 and 2010, while in other recent years it has ranked consistently near the top of that same list.[309]

Closely analyzing St. Louis's crime statistics can be a dispiriting experience. The city's incidence (per 100,000 residents) of violent crime is more than 4.5 times higher than the national average—including 7.5 times the national average for murder, 5.8 times the national average for robberies, 2.2 times the national average for rapes, and 4.6 times the national average for assaults.[310] The vast majority of St. Louis residents victimized by these crimes in any given year are African Americans. Indeed, blacks were victims in 502 of the 567 homicides that occurred in the city between 2008 and 2011. Virtually all of the killers, as well, were black.[311]

In 2008, Charles Quincy Troupe, alderman of one

---

[308] http://quickfacts.census.gov/qfd/states/29/29510.html; http://quickfacts.census.gov/qfd/states/00000.html

[309] http://usatoday30.usatoday.com/news/nation/2006-10-30-city-crime_x.htm; http://blogs.riverfronttimes.com/dailyrft/2010/11/st_louis_named_most_dangerous_city_2010.php

[310] http://www.city-data.com/crime/crime-St.-Louis-Missouri.html

[311] http://nextstl.com/2013/01/understanding-st-louis-homicides-2005-2012/

crime-infested ward in North St. Louis, openly advised his constituents to arm themselves because criminality in the area had become so rampant that the police force would be unable to keep it in check. "The community has to be ready to defend itself," Troupe said, "because it's clear the economy is going to get worse, and criminals are getting more bold."[312] In a November 2013 story about life in St. Louis, the *New York Times* interviewed one longtime black resident who, fearful of the ubiquitous violence that surrounded him, avoided going outdoors after dark and regularly slept with a shotgun by his bed. "There's a sense of hopelessness on behalf of a lot of people," the man lamented. Another St. Louis resident told the *Times*: "It's scary, man. Whoever tells you they ain't scared of this life, they [sic] lying to you."[313]

St. Louis's decay is evident also in its woeful public education system. Though the city's Public School District annually spends over $15,000 per K-12 pupil—at least 40% more than the national average—the children (and the taxpayers) of St. Louis get very little in return.[314] The high-school graduation rates of St. Louis students range between about 46% and 60% in any given year—a far cry

---

[312] http://www.foxnews.com/story/2008/12/02/st-louis-city-leader-says-police-ineffective-tells-residents-to-get-armed/

[313] http://www.nytimes.com/2013/11/20/us/in-neighborhoods-like-north-st-louis-gunfire-still-rules-the-night.html?gwh=D7D202615208310C2840856196321249&gwt=pay

[314] http://www.showmedaily.org/2013/09/what-is-the-cost-of-not-educating-students.html

from Missouri's overall figure of approximately 85%.[315]

According to Missouri's Department of Elementary and Secondary Education, which publishes an Annual Performance Report evaluating every school district in the state, the St. Louis Public Schools in 2013 scored a meager 24.6% on a scale of zero to 100%.[316] Further, students in the vast majority of the city's public schools performed poorly on Missouri Assessment Program tests designed to measure proficiency in English, math and science. For example:

- In 87% of St. Louis public schools, fewer than half of all students registered scores high enough to qualify them as "proficient" in English. In 37% of the schools, *fewer than one-fifth* of students were proficient in English.[317]
- In 92% of St. Louis public schools, fewer than half of all students registered scores high enough to qualify them as "proficient" in math. In 39% of the schools, *fewer than one-fifth* of students were proficient in math.[318]
- In 85% of St. Louis public schools, fewer than half of all students registered scores high enough to qualify

---

[315] http://www.stlparent.com/story/can-900-million-help-st-louis-drop-out-rate; http://www.jewishworldreview.com/1012/star102112.php3#.U2A2MGByFWN

[316] http://news.stlpublicradio.org/post/st-louis-schools-score-unaccredited-range-under-new-grading-scale-wont-lose-accreditation

[317] http://www.stltoday.com/news/local/education/interactive-map-st-louis-city-school-test-scores/html_968f94e4-b851-529a-88fd-be036d17fcb9.html

[318] http://www.stltoday.com/news/local/education/interactive-map-st-louis-city-school-test-scores/html_968f94e4-b851-529a-88fd-be036d17fcb9.html

them as "proficient" in science. In an astonishing 62% of the schools, *fewer than one-fifth* of students were proficient in science. In fact, in 31 separate schools the proficiency rate was below 10%, and in 7 schools the figure was a flat 0%.[319]

Atlanta

The city of Atlanta, Georgia has not been governed by a Republican mayor since 1879, the era of Reconstruction. Since the 1960s and early '70s, Atlanta's mayors have not only been Democrats, but "progressives" as well.

Because it is home to the prestigious historically black colleges Morehouse and Spelman, Atlanta has often been seen as the intellectual capital of black America, and the black Democrat mayors it has elected over the past four decades have automatically become important national figures.

Maynard Jackson was the first; he was elected in 1974 and went on to hold the mayor's office for three (non-consecutive) four-year terms: 1974-78, 1978–82, and 1990–94. He is often credited with improving race relations in Atlanta as the city moved away from its segregated past and into its role as capital of the New South that emerged after the civil rights era. Yet he was also a divisive figure who

---

[319] http://www.stltoday.com/news/local/education/interactive-map-st-louis-city-school-test-scores/html_968f94e4-b851-529a-88fd-be036d17fcb9.html

ran Atlanta in the dictatorial manner of the big-city bosses of the American past. In May 1974, soon after first taking office, Jackson stoked racial tensions in Atlanta when he attempted, over the strong objections of the city's white police officers, to fire the incumbent (white) police chief, John Inman. A Fulton County court judge upheld Inman's right to retain his job, but a few months later the Georgia Supreme Court upheld a new city charter authorizing Mayor Jackson and Atlanta's City Council to reorganize their city's police department in any way they wished. This enabled Jackson to undermine Inman's authority and turn him into a figurehead subservient to the newly created "public safety commissioner" authorized to oversee the police, fire, and civil defense departments.[320]

To fill the role of public safety commissioner, Jackson appointed his former college classmate, black activist Reginald Eaves, who had no safety experience. Eaves' attitude toward his new role was symbolized by his defiant use of public money to purchase extra options on his fully loaded city vehicle. When criticized, he said defiantly: "If I can't ride in a little bit of comfort, to hell with it."[321]

Eaves sparked further controversy when he appointed an ex-convict as his personal secretary and instituted a quota system that gave preference to African Americans

---

[320] http://books.google.com/books?id=yaseH2ICEX4C&pg=PA88&lpg=PA88&dq=#v=onepage&q&f=false; http://biography.yourdictionary.com/maynard-holbrook-jackson-jr

[321] http://www.atlantamagazine.com/features/anniversary/scalawag/story.aspx?ID=1454471

for hirings and promotions within the police department. Eventually, in 1978, Mayor Jackson was forced to fire Eaves for his role in a scandal in which certain police officers were allowed to cheat on promotions exams. (Eaves' unethical conduct continued later on when he became a member of the Fulton County Board of Commissioners and took bribes from local businessmen in exchange for ensuring that their projects were approved.)[322]

Between 1978 and 1979 alone, Atlanta experienced a 69% increase in homicides and now had the highest murder rate—and overall crime rate—of any city in the United States. But while crime was exploding, Jackson reduced the police force by 25% between 1975 and 1979.[323]

Jackson effectively presented himself as an advocate for poor blacks throughout his political career, in large part by pressing for affirmative action and set asides for blacks in public works projects and municipal contracts.[324] But in January 1994, as his third and final term as mayor was winding down, a federal court jury cast a shadow over his repeated use of these strategies. In one of the most politically explosive trials in Atlanta history—centered on an affirmative action program by which Jackson's administration had tried to increase the presence of black-owned shops and businesses at Atlanta's Hartsfield International Airport—the jury convicted a former airport

---

[322] http://biography.yourdictionary.com/maynard-holbrook-jackson-jr; http://www.atlantamagazine.com/features/anniversary/scalawag/story.aspx?ID=1454471

[323] http://crimevictimsmediareport.com/?p=938

[324] http://biography.yourdictionary.com/maynard-holbrook-jackson-jr

commissioner and councilman on 83 counts of mail fraud, 4 counts of tax evasion, and 43 counts of accepting bribes from an airport concessionaire in return for favorable treatment, such as reduced rent at the airport.[325]

These proceedings did considerable damage to Jackson's legacy, leaving the impression that the mayor's affirmative action program had been, as the *New York Times* described it, little more than "a scheme to benefit white businessmen, politically connected blacks, and black political leaders."[326] Bob Holmes, a Democratic State Representative from Atlanta and director of Atlanta University's Southern Center for Studies in Public Policy, put it this way in a 1994 interview: "People are going to ask if other minority participation arrangements were really fronts and whether Atlanta's business is conducted on the basis of political payoff rather than competency and efficiency. It casts the image of impropriety and suggests a 20-year relationship where folks were rewarded merely for supporting Maynard."[327]

Holmes's words proved prophetic. In 2002, when an investigation by the *Atlanta Journal Constitution* found that friends of Jackson and his successor as Atlanta mayor, Bill Campbell (1994-2002), had for years received "the vast majority" of contracts awarded by the Atlanta airport which

---

[325] http://www.nytimes.com/1994/01/24/us/2-are-convicted-in-atlanta-in-airport-corruption-trial.html; http://www.nytimes.com/1994/01/05/us/atlanta-watches-nervously-as-corruption-trial-begins.html

[326] http://www.nytimes.com/1994/01/24/us/2-are-convicted-in-atlanta-in-airport-corruption-trial.html

[327] http://www.nytimes.com/1994/01/05/us/atlanta-watches-nervously-as-corruption-trial-begins.html

were supposed to go to the black community generally. In at least 80 of the 100 contracts reviewed during the probe, one or more of the business partners involved had cultivated a relationship with either Jackson, Campbell or both. Further, most of those partners had contributed money to the Jackson and/or Campbell mayoral campaigns.[328]

As for Campbell, this was by no means his only brush with political scandal. Indeed, a seven-year federal corruption probe resulted in the 2006 convictions of 10 city officials tied to his administration. Also in 2006, prosecutors charged Campbell with personally accepting more than $160,000 worth of illegal campaign contributions, cash payments, junkets, and home improvements from city contractors during his years as mayor. Ultimately, he was convicted only of three counts of federal tax evasion.[329]

For many years Atlanta's political leaders—in exchange for the slavish political support of unionized public-sector workers—promised an unending array of unsustainable pension benefits to those employees. Consequently, by 2011 Atlanta's city government owed no less than $1.5 billion in unfunded liabilities on the pensions of its public-sector workers—an ominous figure that forced the Atlanta City Council to restructure the city's pension system so that all police officers, firefighters and city employees must now contribute an additional 5% of their wages to the pension

---

[328] http://archives.californiaaviation.org/airport/msg47607.html

[329] http://www.judicialwatch.org/blog/2006/01/former-atlanta-mayor-goes-trial-fraud-and-corruption/; http://www.foxnews.com/story/2006/06/13/former-atlanta-mayor-bill-campbell-sentenced-to-2-12-years-for-tax-evasio-348548466/

system to keep it solvent.[330]

Political mismanagement and incompetence have had serious consequences for Atlanta's residents, more than 26% of whom currently live in poverty.[331] As with other urban centers led by Democrats, blacks are hit hardest. Among the nation's 40 largest urban areas, Atlanta has the fifth-highest black poverty rate.[332] And according to a study released by the Brookings Institution in February 2014, Atlanta has a greater disparity between rich and poor than any other urban area in America.[333]

As in so many Democrat-run U.S. cities, Atlanta's public-school system has grown, over time, into a bureaucratic monstrosity of waste and ineptitude. Every year the Atlanta Public Schools (APS) system gobbles up some 15,000 taxpayer dollars—nearly 50% more than the national average—for the education-related expenses of each K-12 pupil in its jurisdiction.[334] Despite this investment, proficiency rates for APS eighth-graders in 2013 were a meager 22% in reading and 17% in math.[335]

---

[330] http://www.businessinsider.com/atlantas-huge-pension-overhaul-is-major-win-for-public-pension-reform-2011-7

[331] http://www.city-data.com/city/Atlanta-Georgia.html

[332] http://www.blackagendareport.com/?q=content/end-black-politics-we-knew-it-will-atlantas-next-mayor-be-white-should-we-even-care

[333] http://www.ajc.com/weblogs/jay-bookman/2014/mar/05/atlanta-breaking-poverty-cycle-proves-difficult/

[334] http://nces.ed.gov/pubs2013/2013307.pdf

[335] http://nces.ed.gov/nationsreportcard/subject/publications/dst2013/pdf/2014467XA8.pdf; http://nces.ed.gov/nationsreportcard/subject/publications/dst2013/pdf/2014468XA8.pdf

For about a decade, a cabal of Atlanta educators and school administrators carefully orchestrated a secret campaign to conceal this woeful educational track record—and to enrich themselves in the process. The roots of that campaign go back to 1999, when black educator Beverly L. Hall, who had just finished serving four years as superintendent of the Newark Public Schools, was hired as APS superintendent and hailed as a highly innovative reformer—even as she remained the target of a New Jersey State Senate probe examining a $58 million deficit that had accrued under her watch in Newark.[336]

Under the leadership of Hall who aligns herself with Democratic Party causes[337] and donated money to the 2008 and 2012 presidential campaigns of Barack Obama, the standardized test scores of Atlanta students began to rise—inexplicably to some observers of the troubled school system. In 2008, according to standards set by the federal No Child Left Behind law, every elementary school in Atlanta demonstrated "adequate yearly progress" as measured by student scores.[338] More noticeably, in many cases, Atlanta pupils from poor and minority backgrounds

---

[336] http://focusdailynews.com/oped-beverly-hall-a-classic-case-of-moral-turpitude-against-atlantas-ch-p4239-1.htm; http://www.frontpagemag.com/2013/arnold-ahlert/atlanta-public-schools-cheat-their-own-students/; http://www.nytimes.com/2000/01/15/nyregion/state-bailout-to-rescue-financially-troubled-newark-school-district.html

[337] http://www.opensecrets.org/indivs/index.php?capcode=wsmyx&name=Hall,%20Beverly&state=GA&zip=&employ=&cand=

[338] http://www.opensecrets.org/indivs/index.php?capcode=wsmyx&name=Hall,%20Beverly&state=GA&zip=&employ=&cand=

were outperforming their white peers from wealthier suburban districts on the exams.[339] In recognition of this rather startling trend, the American Association of School Administrators in 2009 gave Hall its coveted National Superintendent of the Year award, crediting her "leadership" with having "turned Atlanta into a model of urban school reform."[340] That same year, President Obama's Secretary of Education, Arne Duncan, invited Hall to be recognized at the White House.[341]

But then, soon after, the *Atlanta Journal-Constitution* examined closely the large gains that APS students had been making in their Criterion-Referenced Competency Test (CRCT) scores and published a series of articles reporting that some of those scores were statistically improbable.[342] A subsequent probe by the Georgia Bureau of Investigation—the results of which were made public in July 2011—found that a significant number of teachers and principals at 58 Atlanta schools had secretly corrected and/or fabricated many of the answers on the CRCT tests, so as to give the false impression of improving student performance.[343] All told, the investigation implicated 38

---

[339] http://www.nytimes.com/2013/03/30/us/former-school-chief-in-atlanta-indicted-in-cheating-scandal.html?pagewanted=all&gwh=7B8B320A9D9EA9CBE348D9500979FF97&gwt=pay

[340] http://jewishworldreview.com/cols/thomas040413.php3#.U2A-jmByFWN; http://www.cnn.com/2013/03/29/us/georgia-cheating-scandal/

[341] http://jewishworldreview.com/cols/thomas040413.php3#.U2A-vGByFWN

[342] http://www.ajc.com/news/news/local/are-drastic-swings-in-crct-scores-valid/nQYQm/; http://www.nydailynews.com/news/national/georgia-superintendent-orchestrated-cheating-scandal-article-1.1303002

[343] http://tinyurl.com/od7a6qs

principals and 140 teachers, making it the most extensive cheating scandal in the history of American education.[344]

Prior to these revelations, many of the educators involved in the scandal had been handsomely rewarded for their malfeasance. Indeed, Atlanta's *Channel 2 Action News* reported that teachers at 13 schools in particular had received a combined $500,000 in merit-pay bonuses in 2009 alone.[345] And Beverly Hall, for her part, had raked in approximately $580,000 in "performance" bonuses.[346] This self-enrichment took place at the same time that the APS was racking up a budget deficit that, by 2014, amounted to no less than $45 million.[347] Following Georgia's investigation into the APS cheating scandal, Superintendent Hall was allowed to resign without penalty in 2010 but was indicted by a Fulton County grand jury in 2013.[348]

Administrators such as Hall have come and gone in Atlanta, but the children remain behind to pay the price for their malfeasance. According to Binghamton University

---

[344] http://www.washingtonpost.com/blogs/blogpost/post/aps-atlanta-public-schools-embroiled-in-cheating-scandal/2011/07/11/gIQAJl9m8H_blog.html; http://www.csmonitor.com/USA/Education/2011/0705/America-s-biggest-teacher-and-principal-cheating-scandal-unfolds-in-Atlanta

[345] http://colorlines.com/archives/2011/08/cheating_atlanta_schools_received_500k_in_bonuses_what_now.html

[346] http://www.frontpagemag.com/2013/arnold-ahlert/atlanta-public-schools-cheat-their-own-students/

[347] http://www.ajc.com/news/news/local-education/atlanta-school-board-must-find-savings/ndcKq/

[348] http://www.cnn.com/2013/03/29/us/georgia-cheating-scandal/; http://www.frontpagemag.com/2013/arnold-ahlert/atlanta-public-schools-cheat-their-own-students/

Professor Lawrence C. Stedman, APS students lag one to two years behind national averages on the NAEP. "At current rates," Stedman writes, "it will take from 50 to 110 years to bring all students to proficiency."[349]

No profile of Atlanta would be complete without mentioning the crime rates that plagued the city at least since the mayorship of Maynard Jackson. Today, the city's rates of murder, robbery, and auto theft exceed the corresponding national averages by 300%, 360%, and 410%, respectively.[350] In 2012, Atlanta ranked as the ninth most dangerous U.S. city with a population of 200,000 or more.[351] The incidence of murders in Atlanta is about the same as in South Africa, a nation infamous for its exceedingly high homicide rate.[352]

---

[349] http://www.frontpagemag.com/2013/arnold-ahlert/atlanta-public-schools-cheat-their-own-students/

[350] http://www.city-data.com/crime/crime-Atlanta-Georgia.html

[351] http://lawstreetmedia.com/blogs/crime/10-dangerous-large/

[352] http://www.theatlanticcities.com/politics/2013/01/gun-violence-us-cities-compared-deadliest-nations-world/4412/